Topics in Modern History Series

GENERAL EDITOR

Ivor D. Astley, *B.Sc.* (*Econ.*), *A.C.P.*
Headmaster, Hardley Secondary School, Hampshire

60°E
90°E
U. S. S.
M
30°N
SINKIANG
AFGHANISTAN
W. PAKISTAN
TIBET
NEPAL
INDIA
BURM
GOA
EQUATOR
Land over 3,000 feet
0
500
1000
MILES
60°E
90°E

120°E
150°E
30°N
0°
MANCHURIA
(MANCHUKUO)
GOLIA
BI DESERT
Vladivostok
SEA OF JAPAN
Mukden
Yalu R.
Liaotung Penin.
KOREA
N.
S.
Seoul
HOKKAIDO
HONSHU
JAPAN
KANAGAWA
Tokyo
BAY OF EDO
Yokohama
Matsue
Tsushima
Hiroshima
SHIKOKU
KYUSHU
Shimonoseki
KOREA STR.
Nagasaki Bay
Fuchow
Peking
Dairen
Port Arthur
Tientsin
Paoting
Tsinan
SHANTUNG
Tsingtao
(Kiaochow)
Yenan
China
Yellow R.
Soochow
HONAN
Sian
KIANGSU
Chingkiang
Nanking
ANHWEI
Shanghai
CHÜ SHAN I.
Ningpo
HUPEH
Hanyang
Hankow
Wuchang
Wuhan
Hangchow
Shasi
CHUAN
Chungking
Yangtze Kiang
HUNAN
KIANGSI
Foochow
QUEMOY
CHINA
KWANGSI
Amoy
Swatow
FORMOSA
(TAIWAN)
PESCADORES IS.
Canton
Whampoa
Hong Kong
Pearl R.
Macao
KWANGCHOWAN I.
N. VIETNAM
LAOS
LAND
CAMBODIA
S. VIETNAM
PHILIPPINES
PENINSULA
ALAYSIA
Malacca
INDONESIA
NEW GUINEA
120°E

JOHN KENNETT

The Rise of Communist China

with a brief history of Japan

OUR WORK WILL BE WRITTEN DOWN
IN THE HISTORY OF MANKIND,
AND IT WILL CLEARLY DEMONSTRATE
THE FACT THAT THE CHINESE,
WHO COMPRISE ONE QUARTER OF HUMANITY,
HAVE FROM NOW ON STOOD UP.

MAO TSE-TUNG

BLACKIE GLASGOW AND LONDON

BLACKIE & SON LIMITED
BISHOPBRIGGS, GLASGOW G64 2NZ
5 FITZHARDINGE STREET
LONDON W1H 0DL

First Published 1970

Revised Edition 1973

ISBN 0 216 89565 0 *Educ. Ed.*
ISBN 0 216 89566 9 *Gen. Ed.*

Printed in Great Britain
by R. & R. Clark, Ltd., Edinburgh

Preface

One of the main aims of this series is to bring history up to date. Unfortunately too many pupils leave our schools with little knowledge of the contemporary world or recent history. Surveys have shown that, for the majority, studies in history ended with the First World War.

In 1963 the Secondary Schools Examinations Council recognized the difficulties of teaching near-contemporary history, but also made the point that . . . *it is generally accepted that the historian has a special, though not an exclusive, duty to lend significance to the contemporary scene with pupils who are about to join a wider community.*[1]

Many of us have welcomed the chances that the new CERTIFICATE OF SECONDARY EDUCATION EXAMINATION presents—including an opportunity to extend the time-span and thus bring into our syllabus topics which are of relevance, and aid the understanding of the world which awaits the new citizens.

At a Conference of History Teachers in London in 1963, publishers were urged to meet a real need for reasonably-priced *topic* books—which could more easily be up-to-date than the conventional textbooks. They could also meet other needs by covering subjects of present-day importance. This series has accepted the challenge. The result is a series of topic books specially written for a better understanding of 'the world today'.

The speed of change in our world is such that even if we reach the end of the Second World War in our syllabus, we are terminating our studies at a point which represents a very different world to most of our readers. The NEWSOM Report reminds us that even in 1945 . . .*The first atomic bombs had only just been exploded; Everest and not the moon was still the summit to be reached.*[2]

Of course, even when dealing with new problems, with modern and emerging nations, etc., we find that the 'roots' go deep. The topic books must retrace the steps for the story to make sense.

[1] *C.S.E. Bulletin No. 1* (H.M.S.O.)   [2] *Half Our Future* (H.M.S.O.)

We believe that the first essential is a clear, readable story—the essence of history; secondly, that the series should also provide useful source material—with suggestions for further reading and discussion.

* * * * *

There is not much point in going to a football match a few minutes before the final whistle: or in taking up a theatre seat during the last scene of a three-act play. In the same way, you cannot properly understand the happenings of today unless you know something of the events of the past. Accordingly, though it is the aim of this book to tell what needs to be known of China in the twentieth century, there is also an urgent need to explain *what went on before* if the story is to be clear in the mind. Of necessity, then, I have given some account of the great days of the Chinese Empire before it came into conflict with the machine-age civilizations of the West. This may help you to understand why Chinese people today look upon the West with suspicion and distrust.

Since, also, the history of modern China is inescapably linked with that of Japan, I have tried to tell some small part of that country's story as well. As things stand at the moment, however, it is on China, with its vast and ever-increasing population, that the world's attention is focused—for China is winning back her rightful position as 'giant' of the East.

Contents

Acknowledgments

The author and publishers make grateful acknowledgment to the following for permission to include copyright material as detailed below:

CAMERA PRESS LIMITED

Mao Tse-tung proclaims the Republic (p. 1). *Terraced hillsides* (p. 4). *People's Liberation Army* (p. 99). *Liu Shao-Chi* (p. 115). *Red Guard Procession* (pp. 116-7).
photographed by Richard Harrington: *Threshing grain* (p. 104). *Commune production team* (p. 106). *Commune doctor* (p. 107).

BODLEIAN LIBRARY

Chinese Printing (p. 8).

PAUL POPPER LIMITED

The Great Wall of China (p. 5). *'Water-wheel' irrigation* (p. 6). *Court trial* (p. 11). *Opium smokers* (p. 20). *Mandarin* (p. 31). *Emperor Hirohito and the Empress of Japan* (p. 37). *Empress Tz'u-Hsi* (p. 51). *Boxer Rebellion* (p. 53). *Dr. Sun Yat-sen and his wife and officers* (p. 59) *Mao Tse-tung, about 1936* (p. 66). *Grinding soya beans* (p. 67). *Pro-Russian posters* (p. 71). *General Chiang Kai-shek* (p. 73). *Loess village* (p. 76). *General Chu Teh* (p. 80). *Five army leaders* (p. 90). *General and Madame Chiang Kai-shek meeting WACs* (p. 94). *Cotton mill* (p. 98). *Girl tractor driver* (p. 102). *Iron and steel industry* (p. 105). *Chinese Nationalist guard* (p. 110). *Lin Piao* (p. 115). *Shanghai* (p. 120).

MANSELL COLLECTION

Chinese Art (p. 9). *The landing of Commodore Matthew Perry* (pp. 42-3).

JAPANESE TOURIST ASSOCIATION

A Tokaido-train (p. 44). *Gihza district of Tokyo* (p. 44).

SUNDAY TIMES MAGAZINE

Economic chart (p. 119).

The 'Bamboo Curtain' 1

PEKING, 1949

On 1st October 1949, in the city of Peking, a man stood on a high balcony that overlooked a vast, open square where nearly 200,000 people were gathered. He was too far off for most of the people to see him clearly, but on the wall beneath him there hung an immense picture of his broad and smiling face.

His name was Mao Tse-tung and he was the son of a Chinese peasant. His home, not so long since, had been a dusty mountain cave

Mao Tse-tung proclaims the People's Republic of China

but, on this day in 1949, he became leader of the largest single population in the world.

Beneath him, the people cheered and waved, then fell silent as he spoke into a microphone. . . . 'The Central Governing Council of the People's Government in China today assumes power in Peking. . . . We announce the establishment of the People's Republic of China.'

It was a historic moment. The words were momentous, for they told of a great new power that had come into being. For Mao Tse-tung they meant the end of many years of struggle and bitter fighting; years of war and revolution, and of harsh suffering for himself and the greater part of the Chinese nation.

Beneath him, a line of heavy tanks came rumbling into view. These were followed by troops in armoured trucks, artillery, cavalry, machine-gunners, and Red Army men with automatic rifles. They were a sign and a symbol of the New China that had come into being.

China is a nation we need to know and understand. The Chinese people make up something like a quarter of the earth's population. China is strong enough to overrun eastern Asia. Chinese scientists have the knowledge and the technical ability to produce nuclear weapons, and the Western nations have been told that the Chinese Government is ready to face the perils and horrors of nuclear war.

In this age of jet-planes and guided missiles all nations are uncomfortably close neighbours. If we are to help in the shaping of history and the making of the future, then we need to understand what has happened in China in the past, and what is happening today. This understanding is our hope, and our key to the future; we shall have it only if we know something of the Chinese people, their land, their history, and their civilization.

THE LAND OF CHINA

China is the third largest country in the world—after the Soviet Union and Canada—and covers almost four million square miles; so big, in fact, that the Yangtze River, in the central region, is 3200 miles long. The very size of the country has always made it a difficult land to govern because of the problems of communication. Even so, the old Chinese Empire, which lasted for many hundreds of years, took in an area larger than the United States.

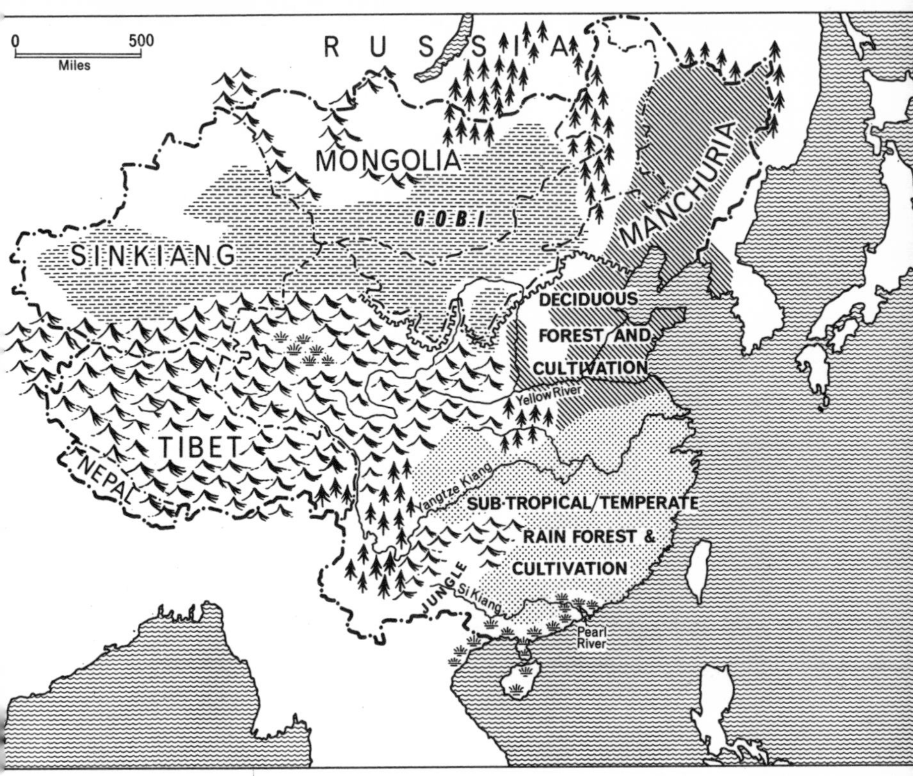

China and the Vassal States: main relief features

What is called China Proper is bounded on the map by a heavy black line, and has the seacoast for its eastern edge. Around the borders of China Proper are the 'vassal states': Mongolia and Manchuria to the north, Sinkiang to the north-west, and Tibet to the west. Although not a part of the empire, Korea was a kind of 'satellite state', under the domination of the Chinese emperors.

In the far west and south-west of China are some of the highest mountains in the world, and the general lie of the land slopes down from west to east. In this direction, also, across the heart of China, there runs an important mountain range, a natural 'wall' that divides the country into two regions, North and South China. There are differences in the language, culture and customs of the people of these regions.

A large part of western and north-western China is difficult country in which to live and the population is small and scattered. Tibet, known as the 'Roof of the World', is mostly high land and bitterly cold for most of the year. Much of Sinkiang and Inner Mongolia is Gobi, or desert. Manchuria, however, is largely a fertile plain, which stretches southwards to join the plains of North China and the rich farmlands of the Yangtze and Yellow River valleys.

Since two thirds of the country is quite unfit for farming, the Chinese people are spread unevenly throughout their vast country, three quarters of the population living on less than one quarter of the land. It is in the plains of north China, the Yangtze Valley, the Pearl River valley (which forms part of the Si Delta in the south around Canton), and the mid-western plain that most of the Chinese people live, and have lived, for thousands of years.

Today the country has to support about six hundred and fifty million people. In this lies modern China's greatest problem. There is a limit to the amount of food that can be grown on her land, which is already under intensive farming. In recent years, millions of Chinese have moved into Manchuria, whose fertile plains are able to feed a growing population.

For many centuries China was cut off from the surrounding lands by her dry, sandy deserts, high mountain ranges and the sea. Only in

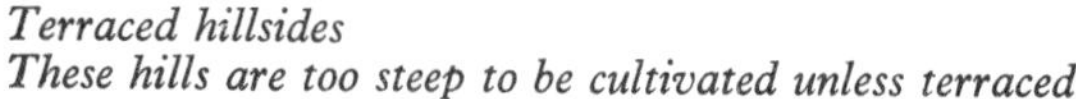
Terraced hillsides
These hills are too steep to be cultivated unless terraced

The Great Wall of China

the north was there a 'gap', and this the Chinese tried to seal with a barrier of their own making—the Great Wall of China, the longest defensive line ever built by man, which ran for 1500 miles across plains and mountains. Even so, the country was invaded many times during the long years of its history.

CHINESE CIVILIZATION

China is the oldest *continuing* civilization in the world; and, for more than a thousand years, the Chinese believed that they were superior to all other people. They had good reason for this. China was the centre of the Far Eastern world. The neighbouring countries took much of their civilization from her. China was first in wisdom and knowledge, which she gave to other lands that could offer her little in return. Her civilization stretched in an unbroken line for some 3000 years, with written records going back to the time of the Shang dynasty, about 1500 B.C. It is true that the records of ancient Egypt reach further back in time, but the civilization of China endured through those thousands of years which saw the rise and *fall* of great civilizations in other parts of the world. She was, indeed, already old and highly-developed when camel caravans, which had crossed the plains and deserts of central Asia, first brought porcelain, paper, and silk brocades from China to the West.

Chinese civilization began in the plains and valleys centred around the Yellow River. Its economic life was based on agriculture and sericulture (the cultivation of silkworms). As time passed, an irrigation system was developed, wasteland was reclaimed, agricultural production was increased in variety, and farming techniques made into a science.

There came into being a system whereby land was rented to tenant-farmers by 'landlord-gentry', who were also government officials and who had charge of tax collection. Taxes were paid to the central government, which gradually extended its rule over the whole of China Proper.

Cities grew and multiplied, and were connected by roads and canals. The daily lives of the people were, for long periods, peaceful

'Water-wheel' irrigation
Square-shaped paddles lift water from the river to irrigation canals

and orderly, and based on the teachings of great philosophers. Scholars were given the highest social positions, and soldiers counted for little in the Chinese scale of things.

The cities were crowded with shops, workshops, business firms, and warehouses. In many of them were big government-owned silk manufactories. Handicrafts, like the making of silk, ceramics, and porcelain made great progress.

With the development of handicrafts and agriculture the volume of trade increased. Big sailing junks carried goods along the rivers. Ships were built, ports grew up, and a commerce by sea began to flourish. The Chinese became a naval people. They sailed in huge cargo-junks to the coasts of India and into the Persian Gulf. There began an economic and cultural exchange between China and central Asia, Persia and Arabia. China became one of the richest and most powerful countries in the world. She offered for sale goods of high quality, fashioned by skilled craftsmen who had a deep sense of beauty, qualities which were not to be found elsewhere. The development of trade made necessary the use of currency; coins were minted by the government, which also standardized weights and measures.

Alongside this social and economic progress, there came great advances in the arts and sciences. A written language was invented, and Chinese scientists discovered the art of paper-making and devised a method of printing from carved wooden blocks. The earliest printed book we know, the *Diamond Sutra*, was printed in China in A.D. 868, about six hundred years earlier than the first European printed books. In the 11th century a man named Pi-Sheng invented a means of printing from movable types.

Over the centuries, Chinese poets and writers produced work which rates among the great literature of the world. Chinese paintings were superb in technique and colouring; architects developed a style of building which was both beautiful and practical. Chinese scientists studied mathematics and medicine, anatomy and astronomy. Eclipses of the sun and moon were observed, and a remarkably precise calendar, which divided the year into twelve months, was brought into use.

For a long time, China had more influence on the West than the West had on China. There was a 'one-way traffic' in ideas and inventions passed from China to Europe. These included methods of casting iron and of deep mining, the breast-strap harness for horses, several types of bridge (among them the iron-chain suspension),

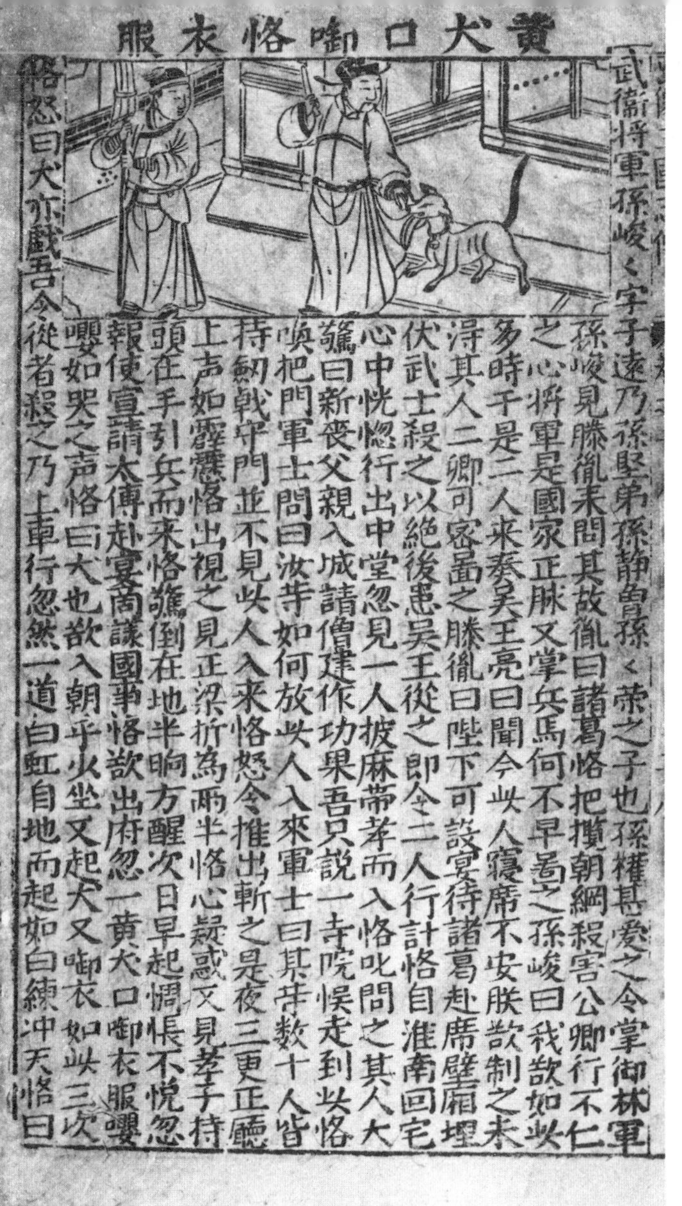

黃犬口啣恪衣服

武衛將軍孫峻々字子遠乃孫堅弟孫靜曾孫々恭之子也孫權甚愛之令掌御林軍孫峻見滕胤未問其故胤曰諸葛恪把攬朝綱殺害公卿行不仁之心將軍是國家正脉又掌兵馬何不早圖之孫峻曰我欲如此多時于是二人來奏吳王亮曰聞今此人寢席不安朕欲制之未得其人二卿可密圖之滕胤曰陛下可設宴待諸葛赴席壁廂埋伏武士殺之以絕後患吳王從之即令二人行計恪自淮南回宅心中恍惚行出中堂忽見一人披麻帶孝而入恪叱問之其人大驚曰新喪父親入城請僧建作功果吾只說一寺院悮走到此恪喚把門軍士問曰汝等如何放此人入來軍士曰某等數十人皆持鎗戟守門並不見此人入來恪怒令推出斬之是夜三更正廳上声如霹靂恪出視之見正梁折為兩半恪心疑惑又見孝子持頭在手引兵而來恪驚倒在地半晌方醒次日早起惆悵不悅忽報使宣請太傅赴宴商議國事恪欲出府忽一黃犬口啣衣服嚶嚶如哭之声恪曰犬也欲入朝乎少坐又起犬又啣衣如此三次恪怒曰犬亦戲吾令從者殺之乃上車行忽然一道白虹自地而起如白練冲天恪曰

Chinese Printing
A page from a Chinese historical novel 'The Romance of the Three Kingdoms' printed from wood-blocks in the 16th century.
Chu-ko Ch'üeh is on his way to a banquet. The dog jumping up to tug his sleeve is regarded as an omen of impending disaster. Shortly after arriving at the banquet he is attacked and killed.

Bodleian Library, Vet. Or. Chin. d. 91, fol. 28v

Chinese Art
A 17th century painting of the Goddess of the Dew by Wan Shou-Chi

mechanical clockwork, the stern-post rudder, piston-bellows, canal lock-gates, and the magnetic compass.

When the Chinese made contact with Europeans, they spoke of them as 'barbarians' and 'foreign devils'. They tried to erect a 'bamboo curtain' between themselves and other nations. Those countries that wished to trade with China were permitted to do so only if they were willing to recognize the Chinese emperor as 'the Son of Heaven, ruler of the world'.

THE EMPEROR AND 'THE RIGHT OF REVOLUTION'

The Chinese people worshipped the reigning emperor almost as if he were a god. He was the head of the state, and his word was law. He could, however, be overthrown if he did not rule wisely and well. This was in line with the teaching of the great Chinese philosopher, Confucius, who held that a ruler has duties and responsibilities to his people. If he ruled badly, then the people had the right to de-throne him and replace him with someone more fitted to the task.

There were many revolts in China. In times of weak government, revolutionary-minded peasants took to the hills and became bandits. Groups of them would then join together under some strong leader who would become powerful enough to take over a whole province. He was called a 'warlord'.

Often, when rebellion toppled an emperor from his throne, the warlords struggled among themselves for power. Private armies ravaged the countryside, farms were destroyed and land left un-cultivated. Thousands of people were butchered or died of starva-tion.

During these times of riot and disorder, the country lay open to invasion by warrior nations living beyond the Great Wall. In the 13th and 14th centuries, the Mongols attacked and conquered China, and set up a new line of emperors. Confucius had taught that an em-peror could be Chinese or *foreign* as long as he was a wise ruler. In the 17th century the Mongols, in their turn, were overthrown by the Manchus of Manchuria, who swept across the Great Wall and set up a dynasty which ruled from 1644 until 1912.

By the year 1800, the Manchus were masters of a great empire. The 'Son of Heaven' ruled over China itself, over most of Man-

A court trial at Canton in 1900

churia, Mongolia, Sinkiang, Tibet, Turkistan and Formosa. Korea, Nepal, Siam and Burma were 'satellite' states. They recognized the Emperor of China as overlord and paid him tribute. This great empire was governed in a way that was markedly different to all European ideas of government.

LOCAL GOVERNMENT

Confucius had taught that politics and government were most honourable professions, which a man should enter only after a long and rigid training. For centuries, no man in China could hold a government post unless he sat a very difficult examination based on the 'classics'—the ancient Chinese writings. This meant that only scholars could become members of the civil service.

At first sight, this seems a fine system, making sure that all officials are men of talent whose ideas have been shaped by fine traditions. Knowledge of the classics, however, did not mean that a man was able to solve the problems of day-to-day government. Neither did a study of the classics lead to original thinking. The system, in fact, helped to breed a class of 'scholar-gentry', who valued the ways of the past as a perfect pattern for living. They wanted things to stay as they were and failed to realize that changes might become necessary when the world itself was changing.

At the end of the 18th century—when some hundreds of steam engines were at work in English factories—China was a land of farmers and craftsmen who were content to use the methods of their ancestors. She was still governed by the 'mandarins', the scholar-gentry to whom the thought of change was hateful. There had been no Industrial Revolution to produce the goods, weapons, machines and transportation on which the West was beginning to depend, and which brought the modern world into being.

China wanted nothing from the West. However, the 'foreign devils' (Europeans), and the British in particular, wanted much that China could provide: tea, silk, cotton cloth, porcelain and lacquer. Soon these foreigners came in great numbers, and they came in ships that were armed with guns. They were more advanced in the arts of war than the Chinese who were unable to keep them out.

Documentary One

Some verses from a modern Chinese song

The sun is rising red in the East
China has brought forth a Mao Tse-tung.
He labours for the welfare of the people.
Aiyayo, he is the people's great saviour.

Mao Tse-tung has a great love for the people;
He is the man who guides us along the pathway.
With him, we shall build a new China.
Aiyayo, he leads the people into the future.

Mao Tse-tung is a son of the Chinese earth;
He will lead us to fight the enemy.
There will come a time when we shall have mastery.
Aiyayo, all our enemies shall be beaten.

Quoted by Robert Payne in
PORTRAIT OF A REVOLUTIONARY: MAO TSE-TUNG, 1961
Reprinted by permission of the author

Extract from a speech made by Mao Tse-tung, 1949

Our work will be written down in the history of mankind, and it will clearly demonstrate the fact that the Chinese, who comprise one quarter of humanity, have from now on stood up. . . . We have united ourselves and defeated both our foreign and domestic oppressors by means of the People's War of Liberation and the People's Great Revolution, and we announce the establishment of the People's Republic of China. Our nation will from now on enter the large family of peace-loving and freedom-loving nations of the world. It will work bravely and industriously to create its own civilization and happiness and will, at the same time, promote world peace and freedom. Our nation will never again be an insulted nation. We have stood up.

Quoted by Liao Kai-lung in FROM YENAN TO PEKING

The People of China

The men in general were well-looking, well-limbed, robust, and muscular. The eagerness of curiosity animated and perhaps improved their coun-

tenances; and they were assembled in such multitudes, that it might, with the poet, be exclaimed,

'How many goodly creatures are there here.'

There are properly but three classes of men in China. Men of letters, from whom the mandarines (sic) *are taken; cultivators of the ground; and mechanics, including merchants. In Peking alone is conferred the highest degree of literature upon those who, in public examinations, are found most able in the sciences of morality and government, as taught in the ancient Chinese writers. . . . Among such graduates all the civil offices in the state are distributed by the Emperor. . . .*

There is a body of doctrine composed from the writings of the earliest ages of the empire, confirmed by subsequent law-givers and sovereigns, and transmitted from age to age with increasing veneration which serves as rules to guide (their) judgement. . . . This doctrine seems indeed founded on the broadest basis of universal justice, and on the purest principles of humanity.

From LORD MACARTNEY'S EMBASSY, by
Sir George Staunton, 1798

2

RIVERS AND SEAPORTS

For centuries the Chinese emperors believed that the only real threat to their power might come from the rebellious discontent of their own people, or from warrior tribes living beyond the Great Wall. They gave little thought to the danger of invasion from the sea but it was from the sea that the 'foreign devils' came.

China has a long seacoast and many seaports, such as Shanghai and Hong Kong. To these, in course of time, came the 'barbarians' from overseas. The first arrivals merited such a description since they behaved like pirate-raiders, seizing key-points which they could use as trading posts or from which they could make forays inland.

China: Rivers and Ports

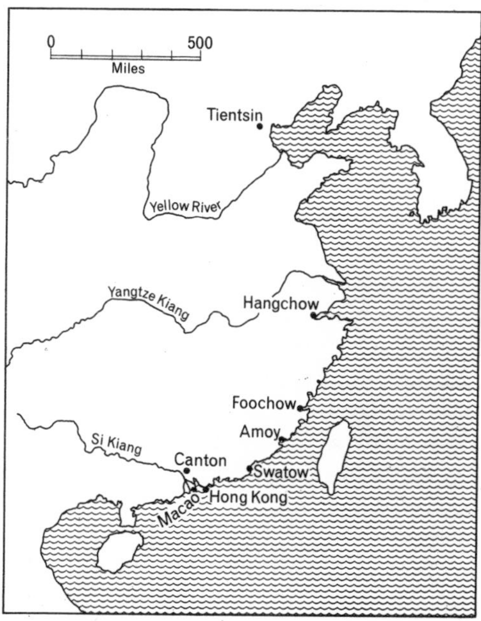

In 1557, the Portuguese claimed the peninsula of Macao, which became a rich trading-centre and, thereafter, a 'launching-platform' for Roman Catholic missionary work. (The peninsula remains in Portuguese hands to this day—a tiny outpost of the West.)

ROMAN CATHOLIC MISSIONARIES IN CHINA

These missionaries were men of good intentions and sound sense who had made a study of the Chinese language and customs, and who were well versed in the mathematics, sciences, and astronomy of the West. They were useful—they knew how to cast cannon, for instance—and were held in some regard by the Chinese emperors.

A certain Father Matteo Ricci, who came to Peking in 1601, was allowed to build a church in the Chinese capital. Further, in 1692 the reigning emperor decreed that Christian priests were free to preach their faith throughout his land.

Christianity, indeed, made some forward steps in China. By the year 1700 it is estimated that there were some 250,000 Chinese Christians. They were, at this stage, permitted to 'mix' their religions, continuing to honour Confucius and to worship their ancestors. In 1742, however, the Pope of the day wrinkled his nose at such practices and declared them to be heathen. Converts were forbidden to do such things. The Chinese Emperor, annoyed that the Pope should give orders to *his* subjects, promptly banned Christianity.

In the long run, the Christian missions in China were unsuccessful for several reasons. The missionaries failed to preach Christ's message in a manner understandable to the common-sense, Chinese mind. The first Protestant missionary did not arrive in China until the year 1807, but soon bitter quarrels started between representatives of the various religious denominations. To the Chinese they appeared to preach contradictory ideas and to be 'anxious to slit each other's throats', as the Emperor K'ang Hsi remarked. The Chinese also judged Christianity by the unruly behaviour of Western traders and seamen, who called themselves 'Christians', but behaved like pirates. Finally, as time passed, Christian missions and missionaries became more and more involved in politics and Western diplomacy.

The message of the West was never really accepted in China because of the contradiction between the teaching of the Gospels and the 'barbaric' behaviour of Europeans. In Chinese minds Christianity was linked with imperialism and 'power-politics'. They were soon to enter into a war with Great Britain, the leading sea-power of the Western world.

'JOHN COMPANY'

The first British adventurer to look for a rich cargo out of China was a certain Captain Weddell, who went there in 1637 with three armed merchant vessels. Defying the orders of the local Chinese officials, he sailed up the Pearl River, where he was fired upon by Chinese guns. His ships' cannon being superior weapons, he had no hesitation in replying with shot of his own. He then put a landing party ashore under cover of his guns and captured a fort. The Chinese, forced to make terms, let him load a cargo of silk, ginger, and porcelain, and so he departed, but we are told he made little profit from his voyage.

By his act of near-piracy Weddell was acting out of turn in the eyes of his own countrymen; he was an intruder, who was treading on the toes of 'John Company'.

In the year 1600, Queen Elizabeth I had granted a charter to the East India Company, nicknamed 'John Company', which gave the Company's ships the sole right to engage in trade with the East. As yet, however, the heavily-armed, private navy of John Company was looking for trade only along the coasts of India.

Once the East India Company had acquired Bombay (1661) and Calcutta (1690), it was eager to 'adventure its goods and ships' from India to China. In 1715, by which time the English people had developed a taste for tea, John Company set up a 'factory', or trading post, in Canton. Here, British merchants and seamen were hedged about with irksome restrictions and looked upon with contempt by 'more civilized' Chinese officials, who thought it necessary to keep a firm control of these lowly 'barbarians'.

CONTROLLING THE 'BARBARIANS' (THE EDICT OF 1757)

In the year 1757, by command of the Emperor Ch'ien Lung, European merchants were forbidden to trade at any port except Canton. It was also laid down that foreign warships, escorting merchant vessels, were to anchor at sea and not come up to Canton; that no weapons were to be brought into the trading posts; that foreigners might not enter the city of Canton, and must pay for all goods in cash; that foreigners must not send letters to Chinese officials, but approach them only by petition sent through Chinese merchants; that, at the end of each trading season, all foreigners were to leave Canton and obtain fresh passports when they returned.

For the time being, at any rate, the merchants shrugged their shoulders and did as they were told. They wanted the China trade and did not, as yet, feel strong enough to stand up against the Chinese on their own ground. Relations between China and Britain were not improved by the failure of two British official missions to China. . . .

THE TWO MISSIONS (1793, 1816)

In 1793, the British sent an official mission to the court of the Emperor, Ch'ien Lung. The chief 'barbarian envoy' was a Lord Macartney, who gave to the Emperor a jewelled box that held a letter from King George III asking for the right to trade with fewer restrictions, and requesting the Emperor to accept a British Ambassador at his court. Ch'ien Lung replied, in lofty fashion, that he had no wish for a barbarian to live at his court, and that the Chinese people had no use for British goods.

Lord Amherst, who headed a second mission in 1816, told the Chinese officials who met him that he would not make the 'kowtow' —three kneelings and nine touches of the ground with the forehead— as a mark of respect to the Emperor. This, he argued, would be to admit that Britain was a 'puppet state' and of less account than China. At this, the Emperor was enraged and Amherst did not even see him, but returned home with his party, all of whom, we learn, felt a deep sense of 'irritation' with the Chinese.

This feeling of irritation was growing. While the Chinese continued to live behind their 'bamboo curtain', big changes were taking place in the outside world. The Industrial and Scientific Revolutions were under way; British factories were looking for new markets for their goods; Britain had become a mighty sea-power, and her merchants were not at all inclined to stomach the haughty attitude of Chinese officials.

The Chinese, for their part, failed, or refused, to see the danger that lurked in the big ships that voyaged from Europe and the ever more powerful guns with which they were armed. The impending war was brought nearer when, in 1834, the British Parliament ended the monopoly of the East India Company. This gave any merchant-seaman the right to trade freely with China. In Canton, the numbers of these men grew. They lacked the patience and understanding of John Company's men, and they were in a hurry to become rich, even if it meant trafficking in an evil thing. Both the British and the Americans had found something that certain Chinese *did* want, and for which they would pay in good silver coins. This was opium.

OPIUM

This is a drug that is obtained from the seed capsules of the white poppy. The Chinese had grown and used it as a medicine for many years, but, by the 1820s, the British and Americans were shipping into China a better-quality opium that was grown in India. It is likely that they also introduced the practice of smoking opium in a pipe, a habit which may do much harm to the smoker, who becomes increasingly addicted to the drug.

Both opium-smoking, and trade in the drug, were illegal. No matter. The traders turned to smuggling the drug, while many Chinese officials turned a blind eye to the trade and grew wealthy from the 'presents' they were given by the smugglers. The leading opium-dealers built fast clipper ships which delivered their cargoes along the China coast. Their trade prospered. By 1839, something like 40,000 chests of opium, each weighing about 120 lbs, were being sold to China each year.

Trade increased until its value exceeded that of the lawful trade out of Canton. Before this time, silver had been pouring into China to pay for tea and silks; now it was flowing the other way into the pockets of the opium smugglers.

The Emperor, growing alarmed at the harm being done to the health of his people and the serious economic consequences caused by the loss of silver, appointed an official to go to Canton and stamp out the drug-trade. This gentleman, Lin Tse-hsü, wrote a letter to Queen Victoria and threatened to invade Great Britain and 'pound

Opium smokers

her people into mincemeat'. Closer at hand, he took more realistic measures.

In March 1839, he ordered all stocks of opium to be handed over to him for destruction, stopped all trade with foreigners, and imprisoned the foreign merchants at Canton inside their factories. By the orders of the British Superintendent of Trade, all stocks of opium held by Britons were given up and destroyed with water and lime.

Commissioner Lin then ordered the British merchants to sign a contract agreeing never again to trade in opium. Death was to be the penalty for breaking this contract. The British Superintendent forbade his people to sign, or to hold any further trade with the Chinese. He began to move all his community from Canton to Macao, and from there to Hong Kong.

Some minor incidents followed. A Chinese was killed by drunken British and American sailors; Commissioner Lin ordered the villagers of Hong Kong to stop the British from landing there; in the Pearl River estuary two British frigates opened fire on twenty-nine war junks, which had sailed threateningly upon them. Four of the junks were destroyed and others severely damaged. Thus, without any declaration of war, began the first of the 'opium' wars.

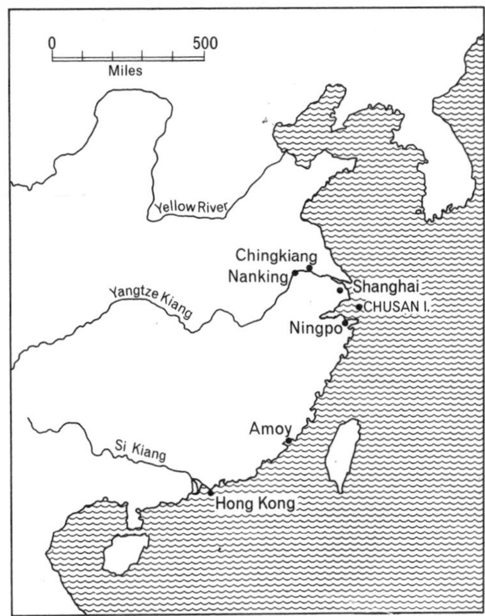

The location of the Opium War

FIRST ANGLO-CHINESE ('OPIUM') WAR (1839-42)

For the first time, China came into violent conflict with a Western power. Her belief in her own superiority was sadly shaken. Her forces, who were mostly armed with bows, spears and ancient guns, were no match for the disciplined enemy troops with their shattering fire-power. The foreigners were, without question, highly skilled in the arts of war, in which they seemed to have had much practice, and most workmanlike in the business of killing.

British forces occupied Chusan Island, Hong Kong, Amoy, Ningpo, Shanghai, Chinkiang. They then advanced on the southern capital of Nanking. On 14th August 1842, a white flag was flown on the city wall. The Chinese Emperor wished to sue for peace. The British had won hands-down.

So there came to an end the so-called Opium War, which the British claimed to have fought to protect the lives and property of their citizens, and which, the Chinese thought, the British had waged to protect opium smugglers.

On 29th August 1842, two high-ranking Chinese officials went on board Her Britannic Majesty's ship *Cornwallis*. They had been sent by the Emperor to sign a peace treaty.

THE TREATY OF NANKING (1842)

This was the agreement that finally opened the doors of China to let the foreigners in. By its terms, China was forced to open the ports of Canton, Shanghai, Fuchow, Amoy and Ningpo to British trade, and to allow British merchants and their families to live in these places. These ports became known as 'treaty ports'. Furthermore, consuls were to be permitted to live in the treaty ports so that they might protect the lives and property of British merchants: these merchants were to be under British and not Chinese law. Only a limited duty was to be paid on British goods, and there was to be equality of status between Chinese and British officials. Additionally, China was to pay Britain twelve million dollars to cover the costs of the war, and the rocky island of Hong Kong was to be ceded to the British Crown.

Defeat at the hands of the British had forced this treaty upon China. The Chinese were angry and resentful. Their resentment grew as, one after another, more and more of the Western nations demanded and were given similar treaties, which the Chinese called the 'Unequal Treaties'.

THE 'UNEQUAL TREATIES'

France and the United States, then Russia and Belgium, Sweden and Norway, all in turn made treaties and received trading rights. The Chinese felt that they had been forced to sign these treaties, and were giving the European nations too much for too little in return. As they saw it, these foreigners had 'gate-crashed' their way into China, introducing unwanted novelties, and were now to be allowed to live in China under their own laws, to rule their own 'concessions' (settlements), and to patrol Chinese inland waters in their powerful ships-of-war.

At the same time that the hated foreigners were pushing their way in, the Chinese people had many hardships to bear. On the administrative level the Government was feeble, the Emperor weak, the tax-system was failing and the civil service was corrupt. Moreover, in 1833 there was a fearful famine, followed by the horrors of the plague. Armed bandits continually ravaged the countryside and, after 1842, swarms of peasants who had taken up weapons to fight against the British, began to vent their spite on the southern towns and villages.

The Emperor had failed to prevent these ills. By Confucian thinking, he had failed in his duty and ought, therefore, to be replaced. Had not the philosopher Mencius said, centuries before: 'It is not murder to kill a wicked king. Such a killing is not the assassination of a ruler; it is the execution of a criminal'?

In China, thoughts like these were in many minds. The time was ripe for rebellion.

Documentary Two

Extracts from a letter sent by the Chinese Emperor, Ch'ien Lung, to King George III of Great Britain

---

Though you, O King, live far beyond the sea, you have respectfully sent to Us a mission. Your envoy has crossed many seas and paid his respects at the Celestial Court. You beg for one of your people to stay at our Court of Heaven. This cannot be; it is not Our custom. The distinction between Chinese and barbarians is most strict. We need nothing from you; We have all things. We do not value strange or ingenious objects. The manufactures of your country are not of the slightest use to Us. We have commanded your tribute-envoys to return safely home. It is your duty, King, to obey Our wishes. Everlasting obedience to the Dragon Throne of China will bring peace and riches to your land. We send as presents to you valuable silks and elaborate curios—all precious things. Receive them with respect. Note the kindness with which We treat you.

This is a Special Edict

Extracts from the Treaty of Nanking, 1842

Article II His Majesty the Emperor of China agrees that British Subjects, with their families and establishments, shall be allowed to reside, for the purpose of carrying on their Mercantile pursuits, without molestation or restraint at the Cities and Towns of Canton, Amoy, Foochow-fu, Ningpo, and Shanghai, and Her Majesty the Queen of Great Britain, etc., will appoint Superintendents or Consular Officers, to reside at each of the above-named Cities or Towns, to be the medium of communication between the Chinese Authorities and the said Merchants, and to see that the just Duties and other Dues of the Chinese Government as hereafter provided for, are duly discharged by Her Britannic Majesty's Subjects.

Article III It being obviously necessary and desirable, that British Subjects should have some Port whereat they may careen and refit their Ships, when required, and keep stores for that purpose, His Majesty the Emperor of China cedes to Her Majesty the Queen of Great Britain, etc., the Island of Hong Kong, to be possessed in perpetuity by Her Britannic Majesty, Her Heirs and Successors, and to be governed by such Laws and Regulations as Her Majesty the Queen of Great Britain, etc., shall see fit to direct.

Article IV The Emperor of China agrees to pay the sum of Six Millions of Dollars as the value of Opium which was delivered up at

Canton in the month of March 1839, as a Ransom for the lives of Her Britannic Majesty's Superintendent and Subjects, who had been imprisoned and threatened with death by the Chinese High Officers.

Article V The Government of China having compelled the British Merchants trading at Canton to deal exclusively with certain Chinese Merchants called Hong Merchants (or Cohong) who had been licensed by the Chinese Government for that purpose, the Emperor of China agrees to abolish that practice in future at all Ports where British Merchants may reside, and to permit them to carry on their mercantile transactions with whatever persons they please. . . .

Article VI The Government of Her Britannic Majesty having been obliged to send out an Expedition to demand and obtain redress for the violent and unjust Proceedings of the Chinese High Authorities towards Her Britannic Majesty's Officers and Subjects, the Emperor of China agrees to pay the sum of Twelve Millions of Dollars on account of the Expenses incurred. . . .

From THE MARITIME CUSTOMS, TREATIES, CONVENTIONS, ETC., BETWEEN CHINA AND FOREIGN STATES, 1917

Extract from a speech made by Thomas Babington Macaulay to the British Parliament, 1840

What does anybody here know of China? Even those Europeans who have been in the empire are almost as ignorant of it as the rest of us. Everything is covered by a veil, through which a glimpse of what is within may occasionally be caught, a glimpse just sufficient to set the imagination at work and more likely to mislead than to inform.

From SPEECHES BY THE RIGHT HONOURABLE T. B. MACAULAY, M.P. 1854

The Taiping Rebellion 3

THE SCHOLAR WHO FAILED

In the year 1834, there arrived in Canton a tall, thin, young man with a slight stammer in his speech. His name was Hung Hsiu-ch'üan, and he was the son of a poor farmer. As a child he had shown some promise as a scholar, and the people of his village had raised enough money to pay for his education. He had come to the city to take the imperial examinations, the key to high position in China.

He failed three times to pass, and suffered a nervous collapse. While ill he went into a kind of trance in which he saw 'visions'. When he was himself again, he read a number of Christian tracts which had been handed to him in Canton. These persuaded him that, in his visions, he had come face to face with God, in the form of an old man who wore a golden beard and a long black robe, and with Jesus Christ, whom Hung called the Elder Brother. He became convinced that God had recognized him as the Heavenly Younger Brother, and had chosen him to set up His Kingdom upon earth. Hung was filled with a new faith. He started a movement that was bent upon rebellion and the conquest of China.

THE 'LONG HAIRS'

In 1847, Hung was moving about among the villages of Kwangsi, preaching his new faith and gathering about him a band of followers who called themselves the 'God Worshippers'. They were baptized, they prayed in their own churches, they smashed idols in their village temples and they let their hair grow long at the back and did not bind it in the pigtail that was a sign of obedience to Manchu rule. Hung had decided that the Manchu emperor was an evil power that he must destroy.

His revolutionary campaign began in Kwangsi in 1848. The 'Long Hairs' attracted to their movement thousands of peasant followers who wanted nothing more than to see the overthrow of the government. The aims of the movement became more and more political. It developed a guerilla army, which became strong enough to attack walled towns.

In 1851, after some minor skirmishing with the Emperor's soldiers, the 'Long Hairs' captured the town of Yunganchow. In its market place, before thousands of his followers, Hung was proclaimed 'Emperor', taking the title of 'Heavenly King'. He spoke of the coming of a new reign in China—the T'ai P'ing T'ien Kuo, or 'Heavenly Kingdom of Great Peace'. All who fought for him, he said, would go to Heaven if they were killed in battle.

There were to be many battles on Hung's road to power.

THE REBELLION

In 1851, the Taiping rebels swept through Kwangsi, falling upon town after town, fighting savagely and meeting with little resistance from the Emperor's forces. As they advanced, they won converts and

The route of the Taiping Advance

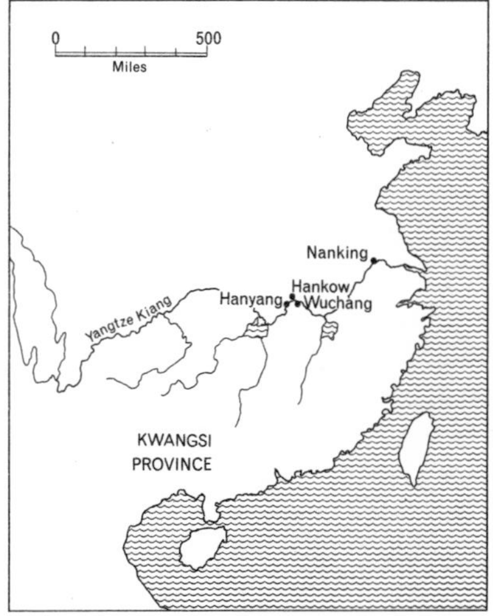

grew in number. They moved north towards the Yangtze Valley and, by January 1853, Wuchang, Hankow, and Hanyang were in rebel hands. Early in March they were outside Nanking, the southern capital. There, on the 20th day of the month, they exploded a mine to breach the fifty-foot thick walls, poured into the city, and butchered the defenders.

For the next eleven years, Hung settled himself in a palace at Nanking, where he led a life of luxury and left the direction of military affairs to the captains and generals he had raised up. The city became T'ien Ch'ing, the 'Heavenly Capital'. The name was ill-fitting. Over the gateways and arches were painted Christian texts but beside them hung the heads of captives, or of those 'God Worshippers' who had broken the strict rules laid down by their Heavenly King.

Even more interesting, perhaps, is the fact that the Taipings made some attempt to put into practice a kind of simple Communism some thirty years before the word and the idea were even known in China.

THE THEORY OF COMMUNISM

In the year 1848, there was printed the first edition of a book called the 'Communist Manifesto'. It was the work of a German-Jew, a poor journalist called Karl Marx, and the ideas it put forward were to have an enormous influence on world history.

Communism, to sum up the idea in the simplest way, means the abolition of private property; the forming of a society in which no one person, or a few privileged people, have separate rights in property; in which there is no inequality and everything is shared among all the inhabitants of a country.

The events of history, said Karl Marx, had so shaped the world that, in all industrial countries, a small group of very wealthy men (the *bourgeoisie*) had all the power because they owned all the 'means of production'—the land, the mines, the factories, the railways, the ships and the banks and everything used in the making and exchange of goods. On the other hand, there were millions of poor people who, in order to live at all, had to sell their labour-power to the wealthy and work for them in their mines and factories and workshops. These people had become an exploited working-class, or *proletariat*.

Clearly, Marx went on, this state of affairs was both unnatural and unfair. The bourgeoisie (or *capitalists*) were the deadly enemies of the working-classes everywhere. A time would come, however, when the workers would revolt and overthrow the ruling classes and set up a world-wide Communist society in which the workers would have control of the government and share in the natural wealth of their country, to the great benefit and happiness of all.

This, then, is the main theme of the 'Communist Manifesto', which was not translated into Chinese until thirty years after the Taiping Rebellion. Hung, however, offered his followers a primitive kind of Communism. This gave his revolt a tremendous driving-force because it satisfied the longings of the ill-used Chinese peasantry.

'All', he said, at the beginning of his revolt, 'shall eat food, all shall have clothes, money shall be shared, and in all things there shall be equality.' He spoke of the brotherhood of man and equality of the sexes. The paying of rent to landlords was to be abolished, and there was to be a new and more just sharing-out of farmland according to the number of mouths in each family. These ideas had the same tempting appeal when they were put forward by the Chinese communists a hundred years later.

In Hung's time, however, most of the reforms were never carried out. Though, for eleven years, he ruled over most of the Yangtze Valley, he was never strong enough to set up a working government outside Nanking. He enjoyed no era of peace in which to try out his ideas of reform. He was finally brought down when the British and other foreign powers with a foothold in China decided to take a hand in affairs.

'CHINESE' GORDON AND THE 'EVER VICTORIOUS ARMY'

In 1860, a rebel army burst out from Nanking, captured Soochow and seemed to threaten Shanghai. This was enough to make the foreign merchants take fright. A force made up of English, French and Indian troops was sent against the rebels, who were driven off. The British lent Major (later General) Charles Gordon to the Manchu government, which gave him the command of the 'Ever Victorious Army', a contingent of Chinese and Filipino soldiers who were led by American and European officers. It is worth noting that they were paid by Chinese merchants of Shanghai. This army, with its foreign weapons and skilled European officers, proved of immense value in the capture of many rebel strongholds. Gordon was a brilliant leader, often moving his troops by river and canal with such speed and stealth that enemy garrisons were taken by surprise.

The decision of the Western powers to defend their treaty ports from Taiping forces, and to ally themselves with the Empire, contributed much to the downfall of the rebels. On 19th July 1865, the city of Nanking, the last rebel stronghold, fell to the Imperial forces. Hung Hsiu-ch'üan had committed suicide by poison some days before. All the defenders of the city were put to death. Any remaining pockets of rebel resistance were speedily eliminated.

It is estimated that 10,000,000 lives were lost during the time of the Taiping Rebellion, through war, famine, or pestilence.

CONSEQUENCES OF THE REBELLION

The end of this time of war and destruction made certain things clear. It had been shown that the Manchu dynasty could no longer control China. The rebellion had been put down by volunteer forces raised by the Chinese gentry and helped by Europeans. The position of the Emperor, Tung Chih, who was then a boy, and his mother, the Empress Dowager, had been further weakened by the expenditure of vast sums of money.

The Chinese gentry—the mandarins, the rich merchants and the wealthy landlords—had upheld the dynasty in order to maintain the age-old Chinese way of life. The peasants in their millions had seen their homes destroyed, and hunger and death everywhere about them. They had gained nothing. It had been shown, however, that a peasant revolt, stirred by the promise of 'sharing wealth', might explode across the length and breadth of China. Eighty years later there came men who made the same promises, and who completed the work that the Taiping had only begun.

THE WESTERN POWERS EXTEND THEIR INTERESTS

Once the rebellion was over the Western powers pressed for further 'rights' to advance their interests in China, their powers of

A mandarin of 50 years ago
His attendants are holding his state head-dress and umbrella

persuasion much heightened by the threat of the armed forces that were always at their backs. One after the other, they secured concessions or settlements in Shanghai, Canton, Hankow, Tientsin, and other cities. Foreigners were given the right to travel inland and full protection was promised, but not always provided, for Christian missionaries, who began to work their way into the provinces; embassies of Western powers were at last opened up in the capital at Peking. Land-areas were leased to European powers: Dairen and Port Arthur to Russia for twenty-five years; Kwangchowan to France for ninety-nine years; Kiaochow to Germany for ninety-nine years; and so on.

Having whetted their appetites in this way, the Western nations began to bite off slices of Chinese territory. The Russians gained eastern Siberia and the Pacific port of Vladivostok. The British and French made their bites in distant parts of the Chinese empire, winning for themselves control of Burma and Vietnam.

The Chinese could find no answer to this challenge. Their leaders disagreed as to the most effective way of meeting the economic and political onslaught of the West. Some believed that China should do all that she could to isolate herself from foreign influences. Others argued that the best course would be to adopt carefully selected techniques and institutions from the West, while another group saw complete westernization as the only possible answer.

And then, in this time of uncertainty, a new enemy arose: one who had been quick to learn Western techniques in war and industry. This was China's close neighbour, Japan. Her attack marked the opening of a new phase in the history of the Far East.

Documentary Three

The Taiping 'Brand' of Communism

In the city (Nanking) the T'ai P'ings were grouped into units consisting of a number of families. Each unit was under the charge of an officer who exercised military, religious and judicial power. Each unit had a common treasury of food and money and a common meeting-place for worship. Surplus food and money had to be given to the national treasury—the T'ien Wang (Heavenly King) was insistent that all property be shared. Remember that the rebels aimed not only at religious change and political power; social reform was also one of their goals. The T'ai P'ing administration of Nanking was in fact a primitive form of Communism.

From THE EXTREME EAST: A MODERN HISTORY,
by Gwenneth and John Stokes, 1964

The Taiping Empire fell, but the causes which brought it into being remained. The strength of the Taipings lay in the visions of the Cantonese. Hung Hsiu-ch'üan (Hung Huo Hsiu) . . . and the social policy which obeyed a classic canon derived from the Confucian Book of Rites. *'All the families in every place will be equally provided for, while every individual will be well fed and well clothed,' wrote the Prince of Heaven; and the social form attempted by the Taipings approached a primitive communism. They destroyed private property. They regarded themselves as people with the mission to share the world's wealth equally among the world's inhabitants, and they used the phrase, 'The wealth must be shared', a phrase which the Chinese Communists were to employ later when they came to name their party* Kung-ch'an-tang, *or 'the Sharing Wealth party'. The remarkable similarities between the programs of the Taipings and the Chinese Communists should not be underestimated: both drew their strength from the same common cause.*

From PORTRAIT OF A REVOLUTIONARY: MAO TSE-TUNG,
by Robert Payne, 1961

34

European 'Imperialism': Extract from a letter written by Humphrey Marshall (U.S. Commissioner in Shanghai during the Taiping Rebellion) to the U.S. Secretary of State.

I think that almost any sacrifice should be made by the United States to keep Russia from spreading her Pacific boundary, and to avoid her coming directly to interference in Chinese domestic affairs; for China is like a lamb before the shearers, as easy a conquest as were the provinces of India. Whenever the avarice or ambition of Russia or Great Britain shall tempt them to make the prizes, the fate of Asia will be sealed, and the future Chinese relations with the United States may be considered as closed for ages, unless now *the United States shall foil the untoward result by adopting a sound policy.*

Quoted by Tyler Dennet in AMERICANS IN EASTERN ASIA, 1941

THE FOUR ISLANDS

Japan, like Great Britain, is an island kingdom lying fairly close to a large continental land-mass. It consists of four principal islands: Shikoku, Kyushu, Hokkaido and Honshu, the most important with the six largest cities.

The rivers of these islands are short and swift-flowing, but there are plenty of good harbours and the people are skilled seamen. The surrounding seas offer rich fishing-grounds. Throughout their history the Japanese people have suffered much from earthquakes, typhoons, and volcanic eruptions.

Japan: showing origins of early settlers

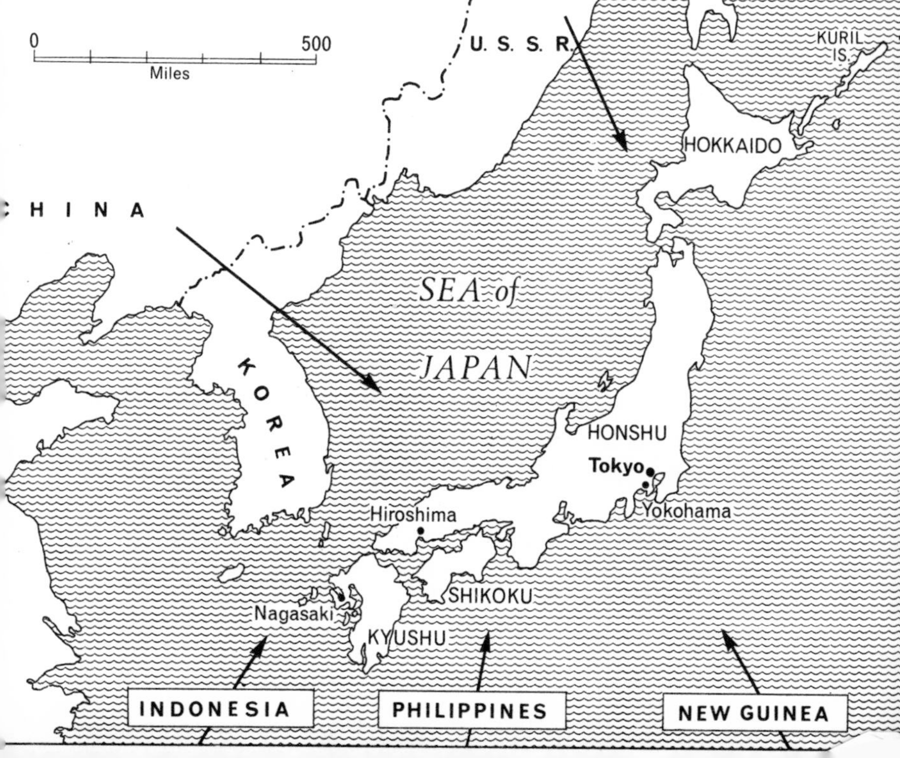

The many mountains of Japan lend charm to the islands but, at the same time, make it hard to farm more than about a seventh of the land. The principal crop is rice. There are few natural resources. Here, then, are two ready-made problems for a modern, industrial nation: how to support ninety million people on the food that may be wrested from so little land; and how to pay for all the raw materials that have to be imported.

ORIGINS OF THE JAPANESE PEOPLE

The first inhabitants of Japan were members of the Caucasian branch of the human family—they were, that is, a white race—and probably came from eastern Siberia. They were called the Ainus. Today there are only about 15,000 Ainus, who live on Hokkaido Island.

The Ainus spread throughout the islands of Japan, but were gradually driven northwards by other migrant peoples who crossed over from the Asian mainland, probably by way of Korea. These migrants were of Mongol origin. They came from Mongolia, China and Korea, but were joined by another stream of incomers who had travelled overland from the south—from the Philippines, the islands of Indonesia, and the Malay Peninsula. It is possible that some of these early settlers came from as far afield as New Guinea.

In the succeeding centuries they spread throughout the four main islands. By the beginning of the Christian era, according to Chinese records, a people of largely Mongol origin had established themselves in Japan.

These Japanese people had little contact, at first, with the Chinese and Koreans. They developed their own language and customs, but had no written language. Like the ancient Greeks, they believed in gods who appeared in human form and who had all the caprices of human nature.

Since no written records were possible, the early story of Japan is made up of mythology, legend, and folklore. According to this mythology, the Japanese Empire was founded in 660 B.C. by Jimmu Tenno, a great-grandson of the Sun Goddess. He bore the title *Mikado*, which means 'Exalted Gate'. From that time, the emperors of Japan were worshipped as gods until January 1946, when the Emperor Hirohito 'came down from the clouds' and renounced all claims to being divine.

The Emperor Hirohito and the Empress of Japan on the eve of Japan's return to full sovereignty

Mikado worship was a part of the Japanese religion called *Shinto*, or Way of the Gods. In this, a deep-rooted love of the homeland played a great part. The greatest honour a man could win was to die on the battlefield in the service of the 'Land of the Rising Sun'.

CHINESE AND KOREAN INFLUENCES

Korea and Japan are separated by a narrow stretch of sea called the Korean Straits. From the 1st century A.D., Korea served as a bridge across which new ideas and a new religion came to Japan.

By the 4th century, Chinese as well as Korean civilization had been introduced into Japan by a stream of incomers from the mainland, who brought with them the knowledge of canal-cutting and road-making, and methods of sericulture and silk-weaving. In the middle of the 6th century Buddhist missionaries in some numbers began to cross into Japan from China and Korea. With them came a flow of Chinese ways and ideas, and Chinese learning and writing were officially established in Japan. The Japanese borrowed much from Chinese culture, in the same way that the countries of Western Europe have modelled themselves on Greece and Rome, but they were not content merely to copy. They adopted and adapted all that seemed good to them, and, in course of time, gave their borrowings a new stamp that was distinctly Japanese.

They did not, however, adopt the Chinese system of local government through scholar-officials. Instead, they developed their own form of feudal government.

FEUDAL GOVERNMENT

Though, in theory, the Mikado was supreme ruler of his land, he was not, in fact, allowed to govern at all. For the most part, he was shut up in his palace, was often poor and neglected, and kept far removed from the scenes of power.

The four islands were divided into feudal districts, ruled by war-lords called *daimyos*, or 'great names'. Each daimyo kept his own private army of *samurai*, 'those who serve', fighting-men who had sworn undying faith to their lord. These had their own special code of conduct called *Bushido*, or 'Ways of the Warrior'. Over the centuries, the soldier remained the chief figure of importance. Craftsmen, merchants, farmers and peasants, counted for little in the social scale.

From time to time, the four islands were given over to civil war when rival daimyos and their armies fought for power and control of land. It so happened, at last, that one daimyo made himself all-powerful and set up as a military dictator. He did not, however, seek to establish himself as Emperor. He took the title *Shogun*, and set up a peculiarly Japanese double system of government. The Shogun was the real ruler, and his position was hereditary, while the Emperor was kept in the background as a convenient figurehead around whom the people might rally.

From 1192 this system of government persisted in Japan, and was the one in force when Westerners first set foot on her shores.

THE COMING OF THE EUROPEANS

In the year 1542, a storm-driven Portuguese merchant-ship, on its way to China, was forced to seek a haven along the Japanese coast.

The crew were welcomed by the Japanese, who were much taken with the 'hollow tubes', which made 'a noise like thunder', and with which these Westerners were armed. Soon, the Japanese were making muskets for themselves.

Thereafter, a rich trade sprang up between the Japanese and Portuguese merchants. The Spaniards, who had established themselves in the Philippines, began to send their ships too, and, in 1600, a Dutch vessel came to Nagasaki. Hot on the heels of the merchants, there came Portuguese Jesuit missionaries and Spanish monks from the Philippines. The Japanese, at first, were friendly to the foreign priests, who made some 300,000 converts.

Gradually, however, the Japanese began to suspect that these foreigners had secret and sinister designs; that they had been sent to prepare for the invasion and conquest of Japan. The Japanese heard, uneasily, of the Spanish conquest of Latin America and the Philippines, and of Portuguese victories in Goa and Malacca. Their alarm grew.

In 1622, the Shogun placed a ban upon Christianity. The missionaries were driven out; thousands of Christian converts were slaughtered or imprisoned. In 1624, the Spaniards were denied entry to Japan, and in 1638, the Portuguese were expelled. The Japanese themselves were forbidden to build sea-going ships or to travel abroad. When, in 1639, Portuguese merchants sailed to Kyushu to try and renew trade, their ship was burned and most of the crew were executed. The survivors were told: 'Think no more about us. Believe that we no longer exist.'

For the next two hundred years all Japanese ports were closed to foreigners. Nearly every contact with the outside world was brought to an end. Only one small window was left open, through which the Japanese might look out upon the world.

THE 'PEEPHOLE' OF DESHIMA

On the islet of Deshima, in Nagasaki Bay, a handful of Dutch merchants were allowed to live and trade; one ship from Holland was allowed to enter Japanese waters each year. For the Japanese, Deshima served as a 'peephole' on the outer world. Through the Dutch merchants, the Japanese were able to import and study Western books and pictures. By word of mouth, the Dutchmen could answer their questions about the West and tell something of its progress in the military and scientific arts.

As time passed a number of Japanese scholars turned to Western studies, particularly after 1716, when a ban on the study of Western books was relaxed. Some of these called for the reopening of the country to foreign trade and for the building of ocean-going ships, so that Japan, also, might search for markets and colonies overseas. Their pleas were ignored. The door was kept barred against the outside world.

In that world, during two hundred years of Japanese isolation, great changes took place; the nations of the West explored and founded colonial empires, revolutions in France and America implanted new ideas of the rights of man; steam propulsion was invented; scientific knowledge and industrialization advanced hand in hand; so, too, did military techniques and the Europeans' ability to kill. Even in Japan, there were changes taking place behind the locked doors.

SOCIAL CHANGES AND DISCONTENT

In feudal Japan, there had always been strict barriers put up between the various 'classes'. During the first half of the 19th century these barriers were slowly broken down. As the population and the towns grew in size, more and more people turned from agriculture to trade and commerce. A class of traders, merchants and bankers sprang up. They were still looked upon with scorn, but their wealth, their power, and their usefulness grew with the passing of the years. They began to use money, not rice as before, as a medium of exchange.

Meanwhile, the daimyo and the samurai, who grew no richer, began to tax their peasants more heavily and demanded payment in money instead of rice. There were years of famine, earthquakes and eruptions. The peasants grew desperate; there were riots and uprisings, unrest and discontent on every hand. This discontent became focused on the Shogun. He was a usurper, it was whispered. Was not the Emperor divine? Should he not be given a chance to rule as well as reign, to make his nation rich and powerful? Had not the time come for Japan to fling wide her doors and take a share in the vigorous new world that had come into being?

As it happened, the nations of the West did not wait for the Japanese to unbar the door and bid them enter. They came with ships-of-war and forced an entry for themselves.

SHIPS OF 'EVIL APPEARANCE'

During the 17th and 18th centuries there had been a number of half-hearted attempts, by the British, the French, the Dutch, and the Russians, to take up trade with Japan. All had failed.

As time wore on, the Americans, who had gained a Pacific frontier, began to send more and more merchant ships to China, and a growing number of whalers into the North Pacific. Occasionally such ships came to grief on the coasts of Japan, or sought shelter, food and water. Their crews were badly used; some, indeed, were placed in cages and paraded like animals before the public eye.

In America, naturally, there was indignation. Even so, the merchants of America were clamouring for trade with Japan, while American missionaries prayed for the opportunity to 'improve' its people.

On 8th July 1853, the Japanese were alarmed to see four 'black ships of evil appearance' steaming into the Bay of Edo (later renamed Tokyo). They were American warships under the command of Commodore Matthew Perry. Their cannon matched their formidable appearance; their commander was firm; the armed force they put ashore was strong and highly-disciplined.

Perry brought with him a letter addressed to the ruler of Japan, from the President of the U.S.A., asking for trading rights and friendly relations between the two countries. He would come back for an answer, he said, within the year—and with an even more powerful force.

This he did. In the meantime, the Japanese had debated what to do. Through the Dutch at Deshima, they had learned of the military might and overseas conquests of the Western nations. They were realists, and saw what they had to do. On 31st March 1854, close to what was then a fishing-village called Yokohama, they signed the Treaty of Kanagawa, which opened two of their ports to American shipping and trade. This was a turning-point in the history of Japan. Soon, similar agreements were made with Russia, Holland, Great Britain and other Western powers.

Even so, the Japanese were still divided among themselves as to the wisdom of letting the foreigners in. Attacks were made on foreign merchants and their sea-port legations. In 1863, there took place a determined attempt to drive out the foreigners and close the harbours to them. A combined naval force of British, French and

Dutch vessels bombarded Japanese towns and forts, put down the rebellion, and forced its leaders to pay an indemnity.

To many Japanese it then seemed that the Shogun, who had failed to keep out the foreigners, was quite unfit to rule. There had come into being a strong party of nobles and younger samurai, who were backed by wealthy merchants, and who wished to give the Emperor direct control of the Government. In 1867, they rebelled against the Shogun. This was the first step in what is known as *The Meiji Restoration.*

THE MEIJI RESTORATION

The revolution was successful. There were battles between the Emperor's party and the Shogun's forces. The Shogun was overthrown. A young Emperor, Mutsuhito, was seated upon the throne of Japan and given complete authority to rule.

Commodore Matthew Perry landing in Japan in 1853

The reign of the Meiji, or Enlightened Government, lasted from 1867 to 1912. In that time, the Emperor and his advisers succeeded in making Japan a modern state, and a power that counted in the world. This they did by walking in the footsteps of the West.

JAPAN GOES WESTERN

Warned by the misfortunes that had befallen China, the Emperor and his advisers saw that if Japan was to survive she must learn from the West and must take to herself all those things which had given the European nations their might and their strength. This, the Japanese set out to do with a most thorough resolution. In April 1868, the Emperor declared; 'Knowledge shall be sought all over the world.'

Large numbers of Japanese students were sent abroad to study Western technology, systems of government, education, law, methods and ways of life. Foreign technicians and experts were brought to

Modern Japan

a) *The high speed Tokaido-Train crossing the Fuji Gawa River Mount Fuji in the background*

b) *Gihza District of Tokyo*

Japan to help modernize transport and communications and to set up modern industries. Foreign weapons and warships were purchased. British naval instructors came to help the Japanese build a war-fleet modelled on that of Great Britain, while the German Army was chosen as the model for military training and organization. Commercial and industrial organizations sprang up: banks were founded; steel, shipbuilding and textile industries were started; a decimal currency was introduced. Cities grew rapidly. All types of communication were developed to cover the huge distances: telegraphic communications were opened in 1869, railway construction began in 1870, a postal system was introduced in 1871, and the newspaper and the telephone made their appearance. Schools and technical institutes were built, and education made compulsory for girls as well as boys.

Japanese law was reformed on Western lines; so, also, to some degree, was the system of government. The real power, however, remained in the hands of the Emperor and his close advisers. The Emperor was supreme commander of the armed forces, with the power to declare war and make peace. His chief advisers, until the year 1945, were always army and navy officers, who were in no way controlled by the civil government.

Inside forty years, the Japanese, with remarkable energy and efficiency, had made themselves a modern industrial power; had grown strong in naval and military might. Japan still had her problems, however. Her population had grown while her industrial revolution was in progress. She had too many mouths to feed, and too few raw materials of her own for her expanding industries. She needed to win more territory in order to dispose of her surplus population, and to find new sources of raw materials. She had seen how the European nations had seized colonies and won empires for themselves. Unfortunately, most of the rich lands had already been taken. Where, then, could Japan look for land and raw materials?

China was the nearest and richest field—and China, as Japan well knew, was militarily weak. In 1894, the new Japan, grown militaristic and aggressive, entered upon a war with China.

Documentary Four

Extracts from the Constitution of the Empire of Japan (1889)

Chapter I The Emperor

Article I The Empire of Japan shall be reigned over and governed by a line of Emperors unbroken for ages eternal.

Article II The Imperial Throne shall be succeeded to by Imperial male descendants, according to the provisions of the Imperial House Law.

Article III The Emperor is sacred and inviolable.

Article IV The Emperor is the head of the Empire, combining in Himself the rights of sovereignty, and exercises them, according to the provisions of the present Constitutions.

Article X The Emperor determines the organization of the different branches of the administration, and salaries of all civil and military officers, and appoints and dismisses the same. . . .

Article XI The Emperor has the supreme command of the Army and Navy.

Article XII The Emperor determines the organization and peace standing of the Army and Navy.

Article XIII The Emperor declares war, makes peace, and concludes treaties.

Article XIV The Emperor declares a state of siege. The conditions and effects of a state of siege shall be determined by law.

Article XV The Emperor confers titles of nobility, rank, orders, and other marks of honour.

Chapter II Rights and Duties of Subjects

Article XXIII No Japanese subject shall be arrested, detained, tried or punished, unless according to law.

Article XXIV No Japanese subject shall be deprived of his right of being tried by the judges determined by law.

Article XXIX Japanese subjects shall, within the limits of law, enjoy the liberty of speech, writing, publication, public meetings, and associations.

Extracts from the Constitution of Japan (1946)

We, the Japanese people, acting through our duly elected representatives in the National Diet, determined that we shall secure for ourselves and our posterity the fruits of peaceful co-operation with all nations and the blessings of liberty throughout this land, and resolved that never again shall we be visited with the horrors of war through the action of government, do proclaim that sovereign power resides with the people and do firmly establish this Constitution. Government is a sacred trust of the people, the authority for which is derived from the people, the powers of which are exercised by the representatives of the people, and the benefits of which are enjoyed by the people. This is a universal principle of mankind upon which this Constitution is founded. We reject and revoke all constitutions, laws, ordinances, and rescripts in conflict herewith. . . .

Chapter I The Emperor

Article 1 The Emperor shall be the symbol of the State and of the unity of the people, deriving his position from the will of the people, with whom resides sovereign power.

Article 2 The Imperial Throne shall be dynastic and succeeded to in accordance with the Imperial House Law passed by the Diet.

Article 3 The advice and approval of the Cabinet shall be required for all acts of the Emperor in matters of state, and the Cabinet shall be responsible therefor.

Article 4 The Emperor shall perform only such acts in matters of state as are provided for in this Constitution, and he shall not have powers related to government.

The Emperor may delegate the performance of his acts in matters of state as may be provided for by law.

Article 8 No property can be given to, or received by, the Imperial House, nor can any gifts be made therefrom, without the authorization of the DIET.

The Chinese 'Predicament' 5

THE KOREAN 'DAGGER'

Across the sea from Japan, aimed like a dagger at the four islands, is the peninsula of Korea. Since the 17th century this country had been a 'satellite' state of China. It was soon to become a 20th century battleground.

Korea lies midway between China and Japan, and Japan and Asiatic Russia. The military advisers of the Mikado looked at Korea across little more than a hundred miles of sea and saw that it was a dagger with which *they* might strike at China *and at Russia*. They had watched, with some misgivings, the growing power of Russia on the Pacific seaboard. In 1861, the Russians had tried to seize from Japan the island of Tsushima, but had been foiled by British intervention; in 1872, they had established a Far Eastern naval base at Vladivostok; in 1891, there came news of the commencement of the far-flung Trans-Siberian Railway.

The Japanese, brooding upon these things, saw the dangers. There was not enough room for two aggressive nations in the lands that border the Sea of Japan. Sooner or later, the Russian advances had to be resisted. Meanwhile, Korea could serve as a bulwark between Japan and any potential mainland foe.

THE SINO-JAPANESE WAR (1894-5)

From 1876 onwards, Japan set out to 'open up' Korea. She sent warships and landed troops on Korean soil in the manner adopted by Commodore Perry some twenty years before. The Koreans, as frightened and impressed as the Japanese had once been, agreed to give Japan trading rights and to exchange diplomats.

From that moment on, Japanese traders came in large numbers to Korea, and, after 1882, Japanese troops were stationed in Seoul for the 'protection' of their legation. The Chinese also had a garrison in the capital. Over the years there were a number of 'incidents'; the Japanese legation was twice set on fire; there were skirmishes with Chinese troops. The Koreans themselves were torn two ways: there was a pro-Chinese party and a pro-Japanese party, and a bitter rivalry between the two.

In the spring of 1894, a rebellion took place in Korea. The King, whose troops were defeated by the rebels, asked the Chinese to restore order. In June, China sent 3000 men to Korea. Japan, though not asked to do so, sent 18000 well-equipped troops, all eager to prove themselves in battle. The dangers of such a situation are obvious.

In July, the Japanese seized and imprisoned several members of the Korean royal family, and placed a puppet regent on the throne. He asked the Japanese to expel the Chinese troops. They, in their turn, warned China to send no further forces.

On 25th July, a Japanese warship torpedoed a merchant vessel carrying Chinese troops. It sank, with great loss of life. The Korean regent at once declared war on China. On 1st August, China and Japan declared war on each other.

The outcome was hardly in doubt. Although by then China had built up a navy and trained some troops on Western lines, her forces were sadly short of ammunition and equipment. Small wonder, then, that Japanese warships defeated the Chinese fleet in a battle fought at the mouth of the Yalu River in September 1894; that the Chinese army was beaten out of Korea; that the Japanese were able to cross the Yalu, march rapidly across Manchuria, and take Port Arthur, where the Chinese had a naval base. The possession of Port Arthur threatened the capital, Peking, so it was not surprising, that the Chinese asked for peace—at any price—and in April 1895, signed the Treaty of Shimonoseki.

TREATY OF SHIMONOSEKI (APRIL 1895)

For China, the terms of the treaty were very harsh. Among other things it provided that:

1. Korea should be recognized as an independent state.
2. China should cede Formosa and the Pescadores to Japan.
3. Japanese traders should have the right of entry to Shasi, Chungking, Soochow and Hangchow.

4. China was to cede the Liaotung Peninsula, with Port Arthur, to Japan.

So Japan triumphed and profited from her first trial of 'expansionism'. She gained much prestige from her victory, but her feelings of triumph were short-lived. Only six days after the signing of the treaty Russia, France, and Germany together 'advised' Japan to hand back the Liaotung Peninsula to China and accept, in its place, a heavier war indemnity. Japan's possession of Port Arthur, they said would be a continual threat to the peace of the Far East.

The Japanese leaders were angry and bitter. They knew, however, that Japan, as yet, was no match for the three Western powers. Resentfully, they accepted that 'advice', but their bitterness smouldered on and was soon to lead to war between Russia and Japan.

THE SCRAMBLE FOR CONCESSIONS (1895-9)

The defeat by Japan had made it clear that China, in spite of her great size and population, was unable to defend herself. There followed a 'scramble' among the nations to win privileges for themselves. One after another, the Western Powers demanded and obtained bases and mining and railway concessions of immense value. Under cover of these leases and concessions, Western business firms began to exploit China on a vast scale.

In 1898, at the height of this 'Battle of the Concessions', the Japanese were filled with furious indignation when they learned that the Emperor of China had granted to Russia a twenty-five year lease of the Liaotung Peninsula. This gave Russia the port of Dairen and the great naval base of Port Arthur—which looked towards Japan. The more imaginative Russian statesmen of the day were against this move. It was, indeed, to prove a fateful step.

Meanwhile, in China itself, an attempt was made to introduce reforms.

THE HUNDRED DAYS OF REFORM (1898)

The Chinese Emperor, at that time, was a young man called Kuang Hsü. His aunt, the Dowager Empress Tz'u Hsi, was a formidable and ruthless lady, who was against all change other than the driving-out of the hated 'barbarians'.

A brilliant scholar, K'ang Yu-wei, and certain other reformers, persuaded the Emperor that it was necessary to rebuild China through a degree of westernization. Kuang Hsü, in a series of 'edicts', or 'commands', urged the Chinese people to study every branch of Western science and learning. He wanted to found schools and an Imperial University; to modernize the army, introduce newspapers for the information of his people, abolish useless court and government offices, have the Chinese take over the running of their own mines and railways. He even, it is said, planned to make a captive of the Dowager Empress.

At dawn on 22nd September 1898, the young Emperor was seized by guards in the employ of his aunt and imprisoned in a palace on an island just outside Peking. There he was treated with contempt by those who served and guarded him, and spied upon by his own wife, who was a niece and great favourite of the Empress Dowager.

All his suggested reforms, except for the creation of Peking University, came to nothing. Six of his reform-minded friends were

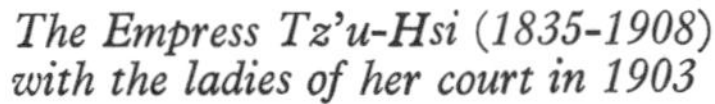
The Empress Tz'u-Hsi (*1835-1908*)
with the ladies of her court in 1903

executed. K'ang Yu-wei escaped and lived as an exile until 1927. The Dowager Empress became the true ruler of China and set her face against change, modernization and reforms of any kind. She ignored the fact that China was no longer a self-enclosed and self-contained civilization, but had become a nation forced to have dealings with other nations; she paid no heed to the voices of the many young Chinese who had been sent abroad to study, who returned and formed revolutionary societies, and who called for a 'new' civilization to restore the dignity of China. Instead, the Dowager Empress lent her support to a movement that aimed to drive out the hated foreigners who had destroyed China's ancient civilization.

THE BOXER UPRISING (1900)

From the earliest times, there had been in China secret societies, which recruited their own peasant armies and made war against the reigning dynasty. Chief among them was the White Lotus Society, which, over the centuries, was always ready to fan the flames of rebellion.

During the two years 1898-1900, the Boxers—a branch of the White Lotuses who called themselves the Society of the Righteous Harmony Fists because they practised a special kind of boxing—rose in arms against the 'long-noses' from the West.

The Boxers wore red sashes and turbans, claimed to have magic powers, and believed that nothing could harm them—not even foreign bullets. During 1898-9 more than two hundred missionaries were murdered by Boxer fanatics. Thousands of Chinese converts also lost their lives. Post offices, railway and telegraph lines, the hated signs of the foreign devils, were destroyed. It became apparent that the Boxers had the full support of the Dowager Empress. Large bands of Boxers, supported by Imperial troops, burned and looted and killed. In June 1900, the red-turbaned 'Righteous Fists' entered Peking, where they murdered a German ambassador and the Chancellor of the Japanese Legation, burned the homes of foreigners, and laid siege to the Western legations. For eight weeks a handful of foreigners held out against the forces of the Boxers and the Imperial troops.

The end of the affair was swift and inevitable. An international force marched on Peking, the legations were relieved and the Boxers

Anti-European posters in Peking, during the Boxer Rebellion

crushed. In August 1900, the Empress fled to Sian taking her prisoner, the Emperor, along with her.

So this anti-foreign drive ended in disaster. Russian and German expeditions, sent to avenge the deaths of their nationals in Southern Manchuria and Shantung, behaved with great cruelty to the Chinese people. Much of Peking was looted and thousands of its inhabitants slaughtered. The Western powers licked their wounds and prepared to make China pay for the damages they had suffered.

THE BOXER PROTOCOL (1901)

This is the name given to the settlement by which the Chinese agreed to 'pay for their crimes'. Its terms were severe: China was to pay an indemnity of about 67 million pounds; a monument was to be erected to the German ambassador, and a Manchu prince was to go to Germany to express the Emperor's regret for the ambassador's murder; a mission of apology was to visit Japan; certain Boxer leaders and high officials were to be executed; the Legation Quarter in Peking was to have a garrison of foreign troops, and other forces were to be stationed along the road to the capital; the allied powers were to be given further trading-rights.

So, at the turn of the century, China found herself utterly defeated by the nations she considered to be barbaric, and forced to know the depths of a new humiliation. In 1900, there were floods and famines that brought misery and starvation to millions of peasants. The imperial government was weak, and was dominated by profit-seeking foreigners who had brought ruin to a civilization that had taken two thousand years to build. The wealth of China was falling into the hands of Westerners, while China itself occupied a most lowly position in international affairs. How should the Chinese people re-build a new civilization which would give them orderly government, a settled agriculture, and in which the arts and sciences might flourish once again? This was the 'predicament' of China.

The humiliation and resentment of the Chinese people were made all the more bitter when there came news of the resounding success of her neighbour, Japan, in strengthening her position in Manchuria and Korea.

THE RUSSO-JAPANESE WAR (1904-5)

A dispute between Russia and Japan over their spheres of influence in Manchuria and Korea led, in February 1904, to the outbreak of war between the two. The war was fought in Korea, Manchuria, and on the Pacific. By May 1905, the Japanese had completely routed the Russian forces on land, and finally destroyed a Russian fleet at sea.

A peace-treaty was signed on 5th September 1905. By the terms of the Treaty of Portsmouth, Japan obtained Port Arthur and Dairen, a lease of the Liaotung Peninsula and railway and mining-rights in southern Manchuria. Furthermore, it was agreed that Japan held a 'special position' in Korea, and had the right to guide and 'protect' that helpless and unfortunate land, which, in a few years, was to be absorbed into the Japanese Empire.

The war had destroyed any immediate Russian threat to China. History was to show, however, that from then on, the Chinese people would have to face up to the menace of Japan.

Documentary Five

The Chinese 'Predicament'

The Russians are spying on us in the north and the English are peeping at us on the west; the French are staring at us in the south and the Japanese are watching us in the east. Our enfeebled China has been lying in the midst of a group of strong powers—and soundly sleeping on the top of a pile of kindling. . . .

K'ang Yu-Wei, 1895

A Reform Edict issued by the Emperor Kuang Hsü, 1898

While China and Europe both believe that the chief aim of good government is the welfare of the people, Europe has travelled farther on this road than we have. . . . Our statesmen and scholars think Europe has no civilization. They are ignorant of the many branches of western knowledge which enlighten the minds and increase the material well-being of the people. My duty as a sovereign will not be fulfilled until I have raised my people to a state of peaceful prosperity. Foreign powers surround us. They commit acts of aggression. Unless we learn and copy the sources of their power, our condition cannot be made right. . . . I command that all my Reform Decrees be printed on yellow paper and displayed for the information of every subject of mine. Let this Decree be displayed in the front hall of every public office in the Empire so that all may see it.

From a report in the 'HONG KONG TELEGRAPH', 1898

Affairs at Peking have now apparently reached the point at which we may expect a lull for the time being, to be afterwards followed by news of the most grave description or assurances that everything has been smoothed over again. . . . It is stated that the Emperor has abdicated, that he is dead, and that he is alive but seriously ill, and so far nobody appears to be in a position to state positively which of the three accounts is correct. We know that an edict has been issued appointing the Empress Dowager Regent, but whether the appointment is to be for good or only for a certain specified time it is impossible to say at present. Events, however, appear to point to a decided victory on the part of the conservative party.

A Boxer Placard, posted in Shantung during the rising

We are forced to practise the I Ho magic boxing to protect our country, expel the foreign robbers and kill the secondary devils (Chinese Christians), so that our people may be saved from suffering. Whichever village you live in, if there are secondary devils, get rid of them quickly. Burn down all their churches. Anyone who tries to disobey this order by hiding a convert will be punished when we come to his place; we will burn him to death. We give you fair warning.

The German Kaiser's Address to his troops on their leaving to crush the Boxer Uprising, 27th July 1900

Let all who fall into your hands be at your mercy. Just as the Huns a thousand years ago, under the leadership of Attila, gained a reputation by virtue of which they still live in historical tradition, so may the name of Germany become known in such a manner in China, that no Chinese will ever again dare to look askance at a German.

The Chinese Republic 6

NEW ATTEMPTS AT REFORM

The Japanese victory over Russia was a turning-point in the history of the modern world. An eastern power had challenged and beaten a western state in war. This fact, said Lord Curzon, a British statesman, 'reverberated through the whispering galleries of the East'.

The effects were felt in China. Japan had shown what China might achieve if only she could set her feet on the right path. Japan had made herself strong by modernization, by following the example of the West. What the Japanese had done, the Chinese now hoped to do.

National feeling ran high; there were demands for reform on every side. Even the Dowager Empress was stirred to take action. She had returned to Peking (bringing the Emperor with her) after the Allied forces sent to put down the Boxer uprising had left the city. She saw that she must change her ways. She even went so far as to promise a programme of constitutional reform.

She was too late, however. Too many Chinamen had grown contemptuous of their rulers. Chief among them, and demanding an entirely new system of government, was a certain Dr. Sun Yat-sen.

DR. SUN YAT-SEN

Dr. Sun Yat-sen, the son of a peasant farmer, had spent much of his childhood in Hawaii, where he was educated at a college founded by Church of England missionaries. He seems to have been much influenced by Christian teaching and Western ideas. Later he studied at Hong Kong, became a Christian and a doctor of medicine.

For a time he practised as a doctor in Macao and Canton. By 1894, he had become a revolutionary. His aim was the overthrow of the Manchus, and the establishment of a republic with a constitutional, democratic form of government. In Hawaii he organized a revolutionary group—the Revival of China Society.

The following year he was involved in an unsuccessful plot against the Government. With a chosen band, he smuggled weapons into Kwantung, arms that were meant to help him seize the offices of the authorities in Canton. A case of guns was located by the authorities, and certain ringleaders caught and executed. Dr. Sun fled abroad with a price on his head.

During the next few years he was active in the United States, Malaya and Japan, preaching revolution to Chinese students and emigrants. It was they who gave money to buy weapons for the revolutionary groups in China. Young men sent to be educated abroad often became revolutionaries. In Japan, where Dr. Sun had his headquarters, there were now many Chinese students. A young man who was studying military science there was much taken by Dr. Sun's ideas. His name was Chiang Kai-shek.

In 1907, there were a number of risings in China, plotted and planned by Dr. Sun Yat-sen: all came to nothing. Ironically, when the revolution *did* come, four years later, it seemed to have no real leaders. Like the Russian Revolution of 1917, it just seemed to happen.

THE MUTINY OF 10th OCTOBER 1911 (THE 'DOUBLE TENTH')

On 14th November 1908, the Emperor Kuang Hsü died at Peking. His aunt was also ill, and died the following day. As her nephew's successor the Dowager Empress had named a child, P'u Yi, then two and a half years of age. His father, Prince Ch'un, became Regent.

In the next three years the unrest and dissatisfaction in China were sharpened by a heavier burden of taxation, by poor harvests, by plague and by flood. The spirit of rebellion was abroad.

A rising had, in fact, been planned for December 1911. Instead, revolt flared up suddenly. On 9th October, the accidental explosion of a bomb in a revolutionary headquarters in Hankow brought police to the building. They found a list of revolutionaries. Among the names were those of army officers in the Wuchang garrison. A number of would-be rebels were arrested, and some executed the following day.

On 10th October, soldiers of the Wuchang garrison mutinied and attacked the offices of the Imperial Viceroy. Shots were fired; build-

Dr. Sun Yat-sen, his wife and officers before their campaign in 1911

ings were set alight; the revolt spread. The soldiers insisted that their colonel, Li Yüan-hung, should lead them—or be shot. He chose to place himself at their head. The rebels captured strong-points and an arsenal stocked with munitions.

News of the rising spread through the southern provinces. Everywhere men seized arms and rushed to join in. In a few days the great southern city of Nanking was in rebel hands.

Dr. Sun Yat-sen was on a lecture tour in the United States when there came word of the revolution. He made haste to return to China. On 29th December 1911, delegates from the rebellious provinces proclaimed a republic and elected Dr. Sun Yat-sen the Provisional President.

The republic was not yet a fact, however; neither was the revolution victorious all over China. There was still an Imperial Government in Peking; its armies still controlled the north and parts of Central China, and at their head was a 'strong man' who was still to make a bid to betray the Republic and keep the old China alive.

GENERAL YÜAN SHIH-K'AI

In Peking the imperial advisers called upon General Yüan Shih-k'ai to put down the revolt. It was he, more than any man, who had organized China's new army. His troops were the best in China. He had little trouble in recapturing Hankow and Hanyang. He then sat back and waited, while province after province fell into rebel hands. On 6th December, the Regent 'retired'; on the next day the Empress Dowager Lung Yu gave Yüan full powers to negotiate a settlement with the rebels. This fitted in beautifully with Yüan's plans.

Both he and Dr. Sun Yat-sen knew that North China was not likely to accept the rule of a government headed by Dr. Sun, a Cantonese and a southerner. Dr. Sun knew also that China could not be turned into a democracy overnight: that there would have to be a period of military government before the whole country could be won over to the revolutionary cause. He agreed, therefore, that if Yüan supported the Republic he would resign in his favour.

On 12th February 1912, the child-Emperor abdicated. Three days later Yüan was made Provisional President of the Republic of China. He refused, however, to make Nanking the centre of his government. He preferred to remain in Peking, the hub of his military power.

His National Army was not strong enough to defeat the 'private armies' of the many warlords who, after the fall of the Imperial Government, seized and ruled much of the countryside as they saw fit. Yüan won their support by making them 'military governors' of their provinces. They, who had little regard for law and order, were willing to recognize and 'play along' with his Central Government in return.

Yüan, it became abundantly clear, meant to strangle the infant Republic before it was very old. He was ruthless and treacherous; all who stood in his path were removed by assassination. He showed himself in his true colours when, in 1913, he drove Dr. Sun Yat-sen from China and outlawed his movement.

THE KUOMINTANG (NATIONAL PEOPLE'S PARTY)

During 1912 Dr. Sun and his supporters re-named their movement the Kuomintang, or National People's Party: a name, and a party, that was to play a large part in the history of 20th century China.

Members of the Kuomintang were soon in open conflict with Yüan. They raised a revolt in the south—often called the Second Revolution. The revolt was crushed; Yüan declared the Kuomintang illegal; Dr. Sun Yat-sen was forced to flee, once more, to Japan.

Yüan now chose his own men to help him govern. He was appointed President for a term of ten years, and then for life. He ruled, in fact, as a dictator. Even this was not enough, however. He planned to make himself Emperor. He failed to do so because of the Japanese who, once again, invaded Chinese soil.

THE TWENTY-ONE DEMANDS

When, in 1914, the First World War began in Europe, China declared herself neutral. Japan, however, as an ally of Great Britain, declared war on Germany, and demanded that the Germans surrender *to her* their settlement of Kiachow, in the Shantung Province of China, 'with a view to its eventual restoration to China'. Tsingtao, the port of Kiachow, was besieged by Japanese troops and naval forces, and surrendered in 1914. The troops remained in occupation; the Japanese declared that all rights enjoyed by the Germans in Shantung had now passed to them.

The Japanese went further and presented to Yüan Shih-k'ai, on 18th January 1915, the 'Twenty-one Demands'. These asked for joint control of the largest ironworks in China, and virtual control over Shantung, South Manchuria and eastern Inner Mongolia. Additionally, China was called upon to make use of Japanese advisers in political, military and financial matters; to undertake to buy at least half their munitions from Japan, to allow Japan control of certain mines and railways, and to accept joint administration of the police in strategic areas. Japan was seeking to control China's affairs.

Yüan accepted the demands. Since China had no allies to whom she might turn for help, he had little choice. Agreement with Japan was reached on 9th May 1915—a day which has become known in Chinese history as the Day of Humiliation. In all the cities of China there were furious protests against the action of Japan, and against the Government of China for giving way.

Against this background of public anger, Yüan persisted in his plan to make himself Emperor. It was not to be, however. In the face of a storm of criticism and hostility, he was realist enough to give up his ambition. In March 1916, he issued a proclamation saying that China would, after all, remain a republic. He died three months later.

THE WARLORDS

After Yüan's death, a warlord called Tuan Chi Jui made himself Premier, with a puppet President, and declared war on Germany and Austria in August 1917. Apart from seizing German shipping in her ports, and sending some 200,000 labourers to dig trenches in France, China could provide no military assistance.

For a decade after the death of Yüan, China was to have 'governments' of one kind or another; and more than once, indeed, she was to have more than one ruling body at the same time. Dr. Sun Yat-sen was to return and hold some sway. The Republic had come into being, but democracy was still far away. For the next fifteen years, China was given over to the warlords, who fought each other for control of Peking and the government of their land.

Documentary Six

Edict, issued in the name of the Emperor Kuang Hsü, by the Empress Dowager, January 1901

All human rules must be subject to alteration. It is not foolish to put fresh strings in a musical instrument; nor is it unwise to change laws made by men. When necessary, our ancestors introduced changes. Most laws in time become out of date. Since the removal of the court, the Empress Dowager has burned with anxiety and we have bitterly reproached ourselves for permitting the abuses that have led China into such peril. Peace negotiations have commenced. The entire system of government must be reorganized so that China will again be rich and strong. The Empress Dowager has stressed the urgent need to adopt the good methods followed in other lands. Our past errors will help us to act more wisely in the future. From 1897-8 there have been many plans for reform. The harm done by K'ang Yu Wei and his rebels was greater than that caused by the Boxers, the dealers in magic. Even now K'ang and his friends are preaching treason in lands across the seas. K'ang and his allies were revolutionaries, not reformers. The Empress Dowager has ordered that we must with all our might work for thorough reforms. We must no longer distinguish between Chinese ways and foreign ways. So far we have copied only the outer clothes of the West. We must go further. We must revise ancient methods, stamp out abuses in our system of government and reform completely. When reforms are introduced, it will be essential to choose honourable and competent men for public office.

Extracts from a letter written by Madame Grenier, wife of the Belgian Ambassador to the Imperial Court of China at Peking in 1907, and describing an audience with the Empress.

Peking, December 1907

Darling Mother,

...Now I'll tell you about our audience with the Empress Tze-Hsi. We started from the Legation at 11 o'clock in the morning—Beric, I, and the Secretary's wife, each of us carried in a sedan chair by four men and escorted by the soldiers of our Legation guard on horseback, and with a few outriders from the Palace, who were seated on very dirty, shaggy white ponies. In front of the first palace entrance, Chinese troops were lined up on each side, not many. Here our Legation Guard stopped and we entered the famous Forbidden City with something like emotion.

. . . *We wandered, in our sedan chairs, in and out of courtyards, irregular buildings that have no windows, and stopped at last in an open space, where we had to get out of our big sedan chairs and get in to small chairs each carried by two men only. Everywhere we saw groups of Chinese officials in various smart clothes and uniforms. They gaped at us when we passed. At last we stopped and proceeded on foot, through a portico into another courtyard, where we were met by three important persons: Yuan-Chi-Kai (Yuan Shih Kai), Natung and Lien-Fang. Yuan-Chi-Kai, a self-made man, short and fattish, is the one who prevented the young Emperor from carrying out his* coup d'état *when he tried to emancipate himself from the tyranny of his aunt the Empress Dowager and was made a prisoner. Yuan is now in great favour. But rumours floating about say his rival, Tchan Tchi Tung will win the day (I don't know if I write these Chinese names correctly). These three important persons were surrounded by a numerous 'suite' and with them we entered a small building, where tea and champagne were served to us. . . . We talked through interpreters and exchanged compliments. . . . Very soon . . . the ladies of the Legation arrived, and were immediately marshalled off with the Minister to the hall where the Empress was expecting them. After about ten minutes, it was our turn . . . and we entered a dark hall where we saw or rather guessed the Empress's presence. The only light came from the large doors that led into it, and which were thrown wide open. In dead silence we walked straight up to the end of the hall, where sat the Empress on her throne, and in the semi-darkness I could feel her fixed gaze and that of the Emperor—some wonderful, mysterious, distant idols gaping at a few modern barbarians. . . . I made one low curtsy at the door, one more in the middle of the roomy hall and still another at the foot of the raised dais on which sat the two sovereigns, motionless like two idols; their eyes alone were alive and piercing and wandered all over our persons. The Empress was seated in the centre of the dais, at her back a tall carved wooden screen and at each side of her a pyramid of coloured apples in china vases. . . .*

The Emperor sat at right angles from his awe-inspiring aunt on a small chair but not near her at all. He looked so young and frail and I felt so sorry for him to be treated like that. . . .

The Empress sat as if she was made of stone, in a black satin dress very much embroidered in gold, that showed off her thin, long, wizened face, with its piercing, glassy eyes. . . . She never moved while Beric's speech was followed by the translation through the Legation interpreter. . . . The feeling that we were standing in front of idols grew stronger. . . .

Then Lien-Fang, on our left, read the same speech all over again in French. . . . Then we mounted the three steps of the dais and stood in front of the table, I making two more deep curtsies. This was the signal for the Empress to give a sign of life. She took a sheet of paper and, in a whisper, read a question to Lien-Fang, kneeling beside her.

He got up, came to me and translated the question into French; my answer was repeated to the Empress in Chinese, of course, Lien-Fang again kneeling. And so it went on, for every question and answer, this kneeling and getting up continually. . . . Then she stretched out her tiny hand and I squeezed it weakly, for each fingernail was encased in a long golden sheath to protect those imperial extremities from the touch of our European hands. It felt like squeezing four pencils. But . . . it is a sign of high rank.

From the letter quoted in THE SUNDAY TIMES MAGAZINE, 3rd October 1965
Reprinted by permission of Mr. Michelangelo Durazzo

THE YOUNG MAO (b. 26th DECEMBER 1893)

In the summer of 1918, a young man, dressed in a threadbare gown and carrying carefully wrapped packages of books and newspapers, came to the city of Peking. Along with six other students, he rented a wretched little two-roomed house close by the university, where he found employment in the library, helping to keep the place clean and the books tidy, and where he was able to follow studies of his own choosing.

Mao Tse-tung, about 1936

His name was Mao Tse-tung and he hailed from the village of Shao Shan, in the province of Hunan. His father was a peasant who had improved his lot by trading in rice, and so managed to pay (though with some reluctance) for his son's education. There was, however, little affection and understanding between father and son, and the two had quarrelled so often and so violently that Mao had left his family for good, to become a scholar and revolutionary.

Exactly what *kind* of revolutionary, he was not yet certain. Like thousands of other young men and women in the New China that was beginning to emerge, he had, as yet, no clear-cut political views, but only a burning desire to help his people in their struggle against poverty and want and injustice.

As the son of a peasant, he had worked from dawn to dusk in the fields and gone barefoot in summer and winter. He knew of all the

Grinding soya beans to make milk

hardships that had to be borne by the peasants, and of their oppression at the hands of 'bad landlords'. Unlike the millions of poor peasants who toiled on the land, however, Mao had been given the chance to study the 'new learning' of the West. He had, on paper at least, some knowledge of democracy and its workings; he had read poetry and history, studied political science and military strategy. He had some skill with words himself, and had done work as a journalist and editor. He had organized student strikes and protests and minor rebellions of one kind and another. He was fired with an enthusiasm to see China set her affairs in order. She stood in much need of reform.

A COUNTRY DIVIDED

There seemed, at this period, a grave danger that China would be 'broken into pieces'. In Peking, under Premier Tuan Chi Jui, there sat the Cabinet of the Republic of China—recognized by the foreign powers, at least, as the 'true' government of China. At Canton, in the south, a 'Secession Government' had been set up in 1917, under the leadership of Dr. Sun Yat-sen. This was something of an 'on and off' government since its existence depended on the goodwill of the local warlords, and, whenever their mood changed, and they turned hostile, Dr. Sun's group would go into exile or underground. This happened in 1919, and again in 1921.

Vast areas of the country were divided up among the warlords, most of whom had awarded themselves the title of 'General'. They controlled large armies, ruled over whole provinces, made their own arms and ammunition, and coined their own money. They were, in truth, nothing more than large-scale bandits: military dictators who formed unstable alliances and uneasy friendships, and quarrelled and fought among themselves.

It was these ruthless and ambitious men who had become the chief enemies of China; it was they who had 'devalued' the revolution. How could they be overthrown and China, once more, welded into a nation?

There were patriotic forces working to achieve this end. There were, indeed, thousands of young men and women who, like Mao Tse-tung, were now 'awake', and who began to play a part in shaping their country's affairs.

THE MAY THE FOURTH MOVEMENT (1919)

In the first few days of May 1919, there came to China news that the peacemakers at Versailles had handed over German properties in Shantung to Japan. Moreover, it turned out that the Peking Government, in 1918 and in return for a secret loan, had 'gladly agreed' to the Japanese claims.

A fury of indignation swept through the cities of China. In Peking, on 4th May, thousands of students attacked the houses of unpopular ministers. The house of the Minister of Finance was set on fire, government buildings were attacked, officials were beaten-up, stones were thrown, and there were clashes with police.

Next day the students called for a strike. In Peking the shops were closed, merchants refused to do business, the railwaymen stopped the trains, and youths refused to go to school. The strike spread to Tientsin, Shanghai, Nanking and Hankow. There were student demonstrations in other cities and in the provinces.

The Government gave way. Three 'traitor' ministers were removed from office. The students had won a great victory, and had become aware of their power. More than this, the thinking-people of China were left with a deep and lasting bitterness, not only against Japan, but also against the democratic powers who were willing to 'share out' the land of China among themselves and the 'yellow dwarfs' from the four islands.

This was a feeling that was also forced upon Dr. Sun Yat-sen during this critical period, for he found that the nations of the West would offer him little aid in his attempt to create a democratic China.

DR. SUN YAT-SEN IN CANTON

In April 1921, Dr. Sun Yat-sen, who, for two years past had been 'sheltering' in the French Concession at Shanghai, was elected President of China—that is to say, of the Government based at Canton, whose authority did not extend far beyond that city. Dr. Sun's hold on affairs was precarious. In 1922, after falling out with a warlord, he had once more to escape to Shanghai. During these periods of 'rest' he had a chance to clarify his basic ideas, drawn up in outline years before, which are known as the Three Principles of the People.

THE THREE PRINCIPLES OF THE PEOPLE

The Three Principles (the ideas that Dr. Sun thought should guide the new China) were Democracy, Livelihood and Nationalism.

The Chinese had had no experience whatsoever of 'democracy' as it was known in the West. Dr. Sun said that she must develop her *own kind* of democracy, which could not be brought into being overnight. There must be time in which to educate the mass of the people, to change illiterate peasants into well-informed voters. During this stage when the people were 'learning' to govern themselves, the Kuomintang would have to direct the affairs of the nation; individuals would have to sacrifice their freedom to the interests of the party and the country as a whole. The Kuomintang, in short, must be for a time a military dictatorship.

Nationalism meant freeing China from foreign influences; for her people to find 'unity', to develop a national spirit, and to establish a strong central government.

By Livelihood, or Economic Democracy, Dr. Sun meant the manner in which the nation's wealth should be used to benefit the people. The state, he thought, should have some control over the country's industries, and help in their development. All the people should be guaranteed sufficient food, clothing and other necessities. Moreover, in agriculture, the basic idea should be 'the land to the tiller'—the man who worked the land should also own it, and have the means of providing for himself and his family.

In his early years, Dr. Sun, whose political ideas had been greatly influenced by the constitutions of the Western democracies, had expected that his party would be given much support by the West. He had discovered, however, that the first concern of the Western powers was to keep, at all costs, their own interests and privileges in China. They were ready to help any warlord who promised to protect their interests. Dr. Sun had lost faith in the West. Now, he looked for help from Russia.

RUSSIAN ADVISERS

The year 1922 was a time of failure for Dr. Sun Yat-sen. Armies that he had sent to put down the Northern warlords were beaten back

Poster proclaiming the friendship between the Chinese and Russian peoples (This was before the split between the two countries)

公債

before they had gone very far. He was desperately in need of help and guidance. He appealed to a country that had, not so long since, staged a successful revolution of its own—the U.S.S.R. He sent Chiang Kai-shek, now a young army officer, to Moscow to study the Red Army and to ask for arms, advice, and financial backing.

The Russians replied by sending to Canton in October 1923, a number of advisers, among them a heavily-built man with a drooping moustache. He called himself Michael Borodin (his real name was Gruzenberg), and he was a skilled and seasoned revolutionary. He was to prove of much value to Dr. Sun Yat-sen. Under his guidance the Kuomintang (National People's Party) was injected with new life; a revolutionary strategy was mapped out, and a revolutionary army created. The Kuomintang, in fact, was reorganized on the lines of the Russian Communist Party.

KUOMINTANG-COMMUNIST ALLIANCE

In Shanghai at the beginning of July 1921, there had been held the first Congress of the Communist Party of China. Among the delegates was twenty-seven year old Mao Tse-tung, who had found in Communism the creed for which he had been searching, and who represented the Party organizations in his own province of Hunan, where, for some time past, he had been forming trade unions among miners, railway workers and printers, and had set in motion a general strike.

In 1923, Mao was moved to Shanghai, where he worked in the headquarters of the Communist Movement. In January 1924, the Kuomintang declared an alliance with the Chinese Communist Party, and permitted Communists to join the Kuomintang as individual members. Mao Tse-tung began to work in close contact with the leaders of both parties. He was introduced to the great Dr. Sun Yat-sen, and he also met for the first time the man who was to become his arch-enemy—Chiang Kai-shek.

CHIANG KAI-SHEK

Chiang Kai-shek was born into a well-to-do land-owning family in the province of Chekiang, in the year 1887. He was given a good education, decided in his youth to become a soldier, and was sent to

General Chiang Kai-shek, about 1927

the Paoting Military Academy, where he did well. He then spent four years at the Military Staff College in Tokyo. It was there that he came under the spell of Dr. Sun Yat-sen and joined the revolutionary movement. When, in May 1924, Michael Borodin and the Russian General Galen helped to establish the Whampoa Military Academy to train officers to lead the Kuomintang forces, Chiang was placed in charge. From then on this handsome young officer forged his way to the front of the Kuomintang Movement.

DEATH OF DR. SUN YAT-SEN (MARCH 1925)

Early in 1925, Dr. Sun Yat-sen travelled to Peking to confer with two powerful 'Generals' in an effort to form a National Assembly. He fell ill on the journey and died on 12th March. Chiang was accepted as leader of the Kuomintang, and in the next few years made considerable progress with the revolution.

Documentary Seven

Extracts from DEMISM OF SUN YAT-SEN
Liberty and the Chinese People

If we speak of liberty to the average man . . . he surely will not understand us. The reason why the Chinese really have attached no importance whatever to liberty is because that word is but a recent importation into China. It is understood now only by young people and by those who have studied abroad. . . . But even those do not know exactly what is really meant by liberty.

The Chinese do not know anything about liberty; they are interested merely in acquiring wealth. . . . We have too much liberty, no cohesion, no power of resistance; we are 'loose sand'. Because we have become 'loose sand', we have been invaded by foreign imperialism and oppressed by an economic and commercial war on the part of the Powers. Now we are unable to resist. If, in the future, we want to repulse foreign oppression, we shall have to break down individual liberty; we shall have to form a very solidly organized body, and so to say, add cement to the 'loose sand' so as to make it into a solid stone.

The liberty of the individual must not be too great, but that of the nation must be unrestricted. When the nation will have freedom of action, China will become a strong nation. In order to attain this end, all must sacrifice their liberty.

Nationalism

If we want to save China, if we wish to see the Chinese race survive forever, we must preach nationalism. . . . What is the present standing of our race in the world? When we compare all the races in the world, we see that we are the most numerous, that our race is the greatest, and that our civilization dates back more than four thousand years. . . . But . . . our actual position at this time is extremely dangerous. If we do not promote nationalism and weld together these four hundred million people into one strong race, China will face the tragedy of being destroyed as a nation and extinct as a race.

An impression, by a close friend, of Mao Tse-tung as a youth

Mao was not unusual in appearance, as some people have maintained, with his hair growing low on his forehead, like the devils pictured by old-time artists, nor did he have any especially striking features. In fact I have never observed anything unusual in his physical appearance. To me he always seemed quite an ordinary, normal-looking person. His face was rather large, but his eyes were neither large nor penetrating, nor had they the sly, cunning look sometimes attributed to them. His nose was flattish and of a typical Chinese shape. His ears were well-proportioned; his mouth, quite small; his teeth very white and even. These good white teeth helped to make his smile quite charming, so that no one would imagine he was not genuinely sincere. He walked rather slowly, with his legs somewhat separated, in a way that reminded me of a duck waddling. His movements in sitting or standing were very slow. Also, he spoke slowly and he was by no means a gifted speaker.

From MAO TSE-TUNG AND I WERE BEGGARS, 1959

China under the Kuomintang (1926–37) 8

VANGUARD OF THE REVOLUTION

In the winter of 1924, Mao Tse-tung fell ill through overwork; a cold turned into lung-trouble and he went back to his own village of Shao Shan to rest. During the time that he lay ill, he gave much thought to the problems of the revolutionary movement. As a Communist he had been trained to think that the revolution could only be brought into being by a rising of the industrial workers in the cities of China. This had been the way of things in Russia, the first Communist country in the world. In China, however, there were at that time only some two million workers in 'city-industries'; moreover, the whole history of China showed that it was in the villages that the seeds of revolution were always sown. History made it clear that the revolutionary strength of China lay in the peasantry, and not the workers of the towns.

A typical loess village in the Kansu province

When he was fit again, Mao went out into the fields of Hunan preaching rebellion and telling the villagers how to organize themselves in a great peasant movement that would destroy the hated warlords when the time came.

In doing this, he risked his life. Hunan was then ruled by one of China's most vicious warlords. For Mao, who was both a Communist and a member of the Kuomintang, 'home country' was also 'enemy country', where all 'agitators' were executed. Word of his activities did, indeed, leak out. A price was put on his head and soldiers were sent out after him. In the late summer, he had to flee for his life over the borders of Hunan and back to Canton.

THE NORTHERN EXPEDITION (1926)

In Canton, Chiang Kai-shek was preparing to lead the armies of the Kuomintang against the warlords of the North. This offensive, it was recognized, could not succeed without the help of the peasants. Mao was set to work to find ways of organizing a peasant-revolt. When the Kuomintang forces marched in July 1926, he and other political agents were busy in the towns and villages, urging the peasants and workers to aid in every possible way the advance of the revolutionary army.

That advance was sure and rapid, much helped by strikes and peasant revolts behind the enemy lines. Thousands of troops deserted from the warlord armies and went over to the Kuomintang side. Within three months several powerful warlords were beaten, and Chiang's armies occupied Kiangsi, Hunan, Hupeh, Anhwei and Kiangsu. In November 1926, a Kuomintang central government was set up in Wuhan. By the spring of 1927, Chiang's soldiers were outside Shanghai, with all of China south of the Yangtze in their hands.

PURGE OF THE COMMUNISTS (APRIL 1927)

For some time, there had been a rift in the Kuomintang Party. It had developed a 'left' wing and a 'right' wing. The left, led by a politician called Wang Ching-wei, was ready to work with the Communists and aimed at wide-reaching reforms. The right feared a Communist 'take-over' once the warlords were defeated, and viewed with alarm the force and violence of the recent peasant uprisings and the revolutionary spirit of the workers in the towns, who had attacked the property of Chinese merchants and industrialists and damaged foreign business houses.

In Shanghai, 600,000 workers, mobilized by the Communist leader, Chou En-lai, seized all strong-points and won control of the city. The Communists in Chiang's ranks made no secret of their intention to seize the property of the great financiers of the city as soon as it fell. Chiang was in need of money to pay his troops; and financial backing to further his drive to the North. The time had come to 'drop' the Communists, he decided, and to do away with the threat of a 'Red' uprising in the rear of his advancing army. He came to an understanding with the Shanghai financiers.

On 12th April 1927, he ordered his troops to occupy the city—and to exterminate all of its Communists and their supporters. This was the beginning of a widespread massacre of Communists, trade unionists, labour leaders, and rebellious peasants in Kuomintang-held country. Similar massacres took place in other towns and cities. Those Communist leaders who were able to escape, Chou En-lai among them, went to Russia or 'underground'.

On the day of the Shanghai massacre, Chiang announced that he had taken power into his own hands and would set up a government in Nanking. The Left Wing Kuomintang Government held out until Chiang's forces occupied Wuhan and put an end to its existence. Chiang's power became supreme.

In August 1927, his forces resumed the march on Peking. Again, the campaign was swift and successful. In June 1928, Chiang's troops captured Peking, and China was united under one government.

CHINA UNDER 'NATIONALIST' RULE

Chiang's new Government soon gained the recognition of the foreign powers, to whom it was known as the 'Nationalist' Government. Peking ceased to be the capital. Nanking, the new capital, was in the centre of the country and better placed, strategically.

The Nationalist Government began to inject new life into Chinese society with a programme of modernization. Foreign trade was increased, and the old agreements—restricting the right of the Chinese Government to control its own tariffs—were brought to an end. New railways were built, new factories went into production, and new irrigation projects improved agriculture in certain areas. Modern hospitals were founded, and many new schools and universities were built with government help.

A new constitution, based on Dr. Sun's 'Three Principles of the People', was created, but no real attempt was made to set up a representative government. Chiang showed no real desire to make China a democracy. He kept a tight hold on the reins of power by making himself at one and the same time head of the government, the party, and the army. He brooked no opposition to the Kuomintang, but used the army and secret police to eliminate those who opposed him. To ensure control his chosen men held all the high positions; his financier-friends held control of the national pursestrings; the Government was a party-dictatorship. There was still a rich and highly-favoured minority; land remained in the hands of the landlords, who charged high rents, and the living-standard of the greater part of the Chinese people remained as low as ever.

As time wore on, more and more money had to be spent on buying from abroad the military aeroplanes, the light tanks and the heavy guns that Chiang needed in the ruthless and never-ending war that he was waging in his efforts to wipe out, once and for all, a small but troublesome army of Communist guerilla-fighters, led by Mao Tse-tung.

MAO'S MOUNTAIN STRONGHOLD (CHINGKANGSHAN)

For a time, after the massacre of the Communists, Mao Tse-tung had attempted to fight back by leading peasant uprisings in Hunan. Here he formed a First Peasants' and Workers' Army which took part in a revolt that has become known as the 'Autumn Crop Uprising'. It failed. Kuomintang troops closed in on the area; the peasant forces were surrounded and cut down. Mao himself was arrested, but managed to escape.

He found himself left with an army of a thousand men who had less than two hundred rifles between them. His next step was in keeping with the behaviour of Chinese rebels for centuries past: he planned to set up a base far from the reach of the central government. He led his ragged rifle-regiment to a remote mountain district known

General Chu Teh, Commander-in-Chief of the Communist Armies

as Chingkangshan, on the Hunan-Kiangsi border. On a high plateau about twenty-five miles wide, he found the natural fortress he was seeking—protected by cliffs and hidden among thick pine forests, and linked to the outside world by five steep and narrow paths.

When winter came, it was bitterly cold in this mountain-lair. Food was scarce and the future dark and unpromising. The occupants of this little independent state held out, however, and in the spring they were joined by Chu Teh.

CHU TEH, THE WARLORD REVOLUTIONARY

Chu Teh, who was forty-two years old, came of a wealthy family, had trained as a soldier and risen to be brigadier-general. He had fought in rebellions against Yüan Shih-k'ai. Finally, he had become a warlord in the province of Szechuan. He was also something of a scholar, who studied revolutionary literature and decided to become a Communist. He had travelled to Germany and France, and studied Marxism in Moscow, returning to China in 1925, and working with the Kuomintang. When the Communist Party was driven underground, he, too, led a column of troops to the Kiangsi-Kwantung border. Here, in the spring, there came a messenger from Mao, inviting Chu Teh to join forces with him at Chingkangshan.

THE CHINESE SOVIET REPUBLIC (1931-4)

In May 1928, Chu Teh reached Chingkangshan at the head of two thousand tattered troops. He became the military head of the combined Red forces, and Mao the political leader. Peasant volunteers had flocked to the mountain until the army numbered about 11,000 men. The troops were trained in guerilla warfare. They now had some machine-guns and trench-mortars that had been captured from the enemy.

Although Chingkangshan was only six hundred miles south-west of Shanghai, the lack of roads and bridges, and the wildness of the country favoured the guerillas, who ambushed Kuomintang forces sent against them, or lured them into impassable ravines, then made their attack and vanished again among their forests and their high, steep cliffs.

Life in the mountain-stronghold became more and more difficult, however. Larger and stronger forces were being sent against Mao's guerillas, who could not raise enough food to support their growing numbers. A move had become necessary. At dawn, on 4th January 1929, the Red Army men made their way along a high mountain ridge that ran to the south along the Kiangsi-Hunan border. Day by day they marched across snow-covered mountains, bivouacked in shivering misery on their crests, beat off enemy attacks, and marched once more along the mountain trails. Many died of exposure; food was scarce, and sometimes the army lived on roots.

They fought their way into the pine-clad hills of South Kiangsi, where once again they set up a base in a district that was ripe for rebellion. The peasants were roused to drive out the landlords and to re-distribute the land; to organize labour-brigades and introduce group-farming; to set up village soviets (or councils) to govern the countryside. In February 1930, Mao was made chairman of a Provincial Soviet Government, with the village of Juichin as its capital. The movement gained strength and spread eastward until it took in six counties of Southern Kiangsi and Fukien.

For Chiang Kai-shek it was a dangerous movement—one that might come to embrace the whole of China. At any cost, the Communists had to be annihilated.

THE 'ANNIHILATION' CAMPAIGNS (1930-34)

In the course of three years Chiang made five onslaughts against the Red base in Southern China, hurling huge armies into battles that were fought to stamp out the Communist menace for ever. He failed to do so. He had modern weapons, aeroplanes, heavy guns, well-trained officers and highly-disciplined divisions; the Red armies were ragged, under-fed and ill-equipped, yet time after time they inflicted heavy defeats on an enemy who out-numbered them ten to one. To do this they chose their own fighting-grounds and were kept informed of troop-movements by peasant spies; they made swift and unexpected marches and sudden, surprise attacks; they lured the enemy into traps and fooled him by wearing captured uniforms; they fell upon him at night, hit at his weakest points, captured his rifles and machine-guns, his trench mortars and radio-transmitters, then withdrew into hiding-places among the hills until the time came to make another surprise sally, when they struck back with their captured guns.

From October 1933 until October 1934, Chiang kept 400,000 troops in the field. In his Fifth Annihilation Campaign he made use of 'the fiery wall'. The peasants of the areas surrounding the Red base were either 'moved out' or executed. Lines of entrenchments and fortified blockhouses were built in a ring and the land all round was put to the flame. The Red Army was imprisoned by the enemy divisions and their chain of blockhouses. The enemy began to close in.

Mao and Chu Teh came to a decision. The whole of their Soviet Republic, or what was left of it, would have to break out of the trap and move to safer ground. Their plans were laid; their orders secretly given. On the evening of 18th October 1934, there began one of the most extraordinary adventures of modern times.

THE LONG MARCH (18th OCTOBER 1934—29th OCTOBER 1935)

In stealth and darkness, the men of the Red Army were gathered before a reported weak point in the enemy's 'ring of iron'. They made a sudden offensive and, after heavy fighting and severe losses, broke through the line of fortifications. Hard on their heels came carts, drawn by mules and ponies, carrying weapons, ammunition, food, tools, printing-presses, seed, bank-notes and silver dollars, peasant women and children, and the families of the soldiers. Everything that could be carried, and every living creature inside the Kuomintang Ring, set out on a march that was to last a year and cover 6000 miles.

The route of the Long March

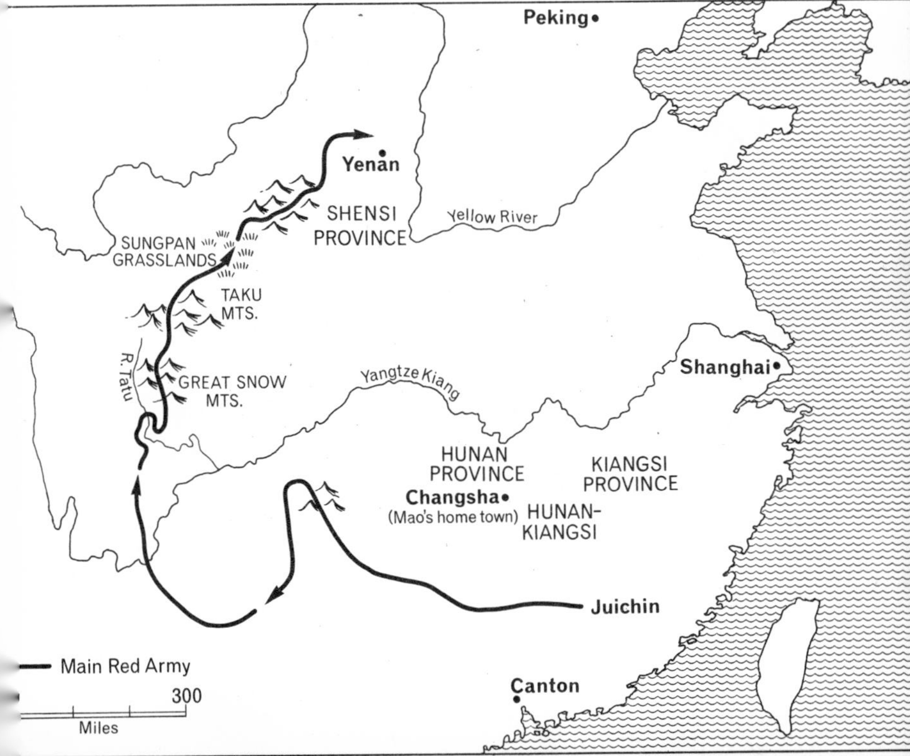

A hundred thousand set out; eighty thousand were doomed to die. For 368 days the Red columns were dive-bombed and machine-gunned, pursued by Kuomintang forces on land, attacked and encircled and ambushed. Chiang Kai-shek never let up in his attacks, but the March went on.

After suffering terrible losses, Mao and Chu Teh led their forces into desolate regions where the enemy found it hard to follow. They swung in a wide arc towards the north, crossing snow-bound mountain ranges, turbulent rivers, swamps and sandy plains, averaging twenty-four miles a day in beating rain, snowstorms, fog and mist, and blazing heat. Finally, they crossed the terrible Grasslands, where a cold rain fell nearly all the time, where no human beings lived, and treacherous bogs were everywhere, waiting to suck a man down if he stepped off the firmer parts. The black mud that oozed up between their feet was foul and poisonous and made their legs swell with blisters, and often they had nothing to eat but roots.

Here, the forces of the Kuomintang gave up the chase, while Mao's men pressed on, through Kansi and on to northern Shensi, to a place called Pao An, a little walled village near the Great Wall of China. The survivors had crossed eighteen mountain ranges and twenty-four rivers; they had fought more than two hundred battles; they had passed through eleven provinces and covered some 6000 miles on foot. They had cut a passage through China at a frightful cost, but these columns of gaunt and ragged men who were the remnants of an army had, with their Long March, sown seeds that would yield a harvest in the future. Moreover, by moving themselves to the north, Mao's guerilla fighters had placed themselves ready to strike at the Japanese forces that were soon to launch an attack on China.

Documentary Eight

The basic principles of guerilla warfare, expressed by Mao Tse-tung in a verse that was recited by his Red Army soldiers

---

The enemy advances: we retreat
The enemy halts: we harass
The enemy tires: we attack
The enemy retreats: we pursue.

Extracts from SELECTED WORKS of Mao Tse-tung
The Peasant Revolution

. . . a revolution is not the same thing as inviting people to dinner, or writing an essay, or painting a picture, or doing fancy needlework; it cannot be anything so refined, so calm and gentle, or so mild, kind, courteous, restrained or magnanimous. A revolution is an uprising, an act of violence whereby one class overthrows another. A rural revolution is a revolution by which the peasantry overthrows the authority of the feudal landlord class. If the peasants do not use the maximum of their strength, they can never overthrow the authority of the landlords which has been deeply rooted for thousands of years.

To put it bluntly, it was necessary to bring about a brief reign of terror in every rural area; otherwise one could never suppress the activities of the counter-revolutionaries in the countryside or overthrow the authority of the gentry. To right a wrong it is necessary to exceed the proper limits, and the wrong cannot be righted without the proper limits being exceeded.

From a report to the Chinese Communist Party

The Red Army, 1928

The majority of the Red Army soldiers came from mercenary armies; but once in the Red Army, they change their character. First of all the Red Army has abolished the mercenary system, making the soldiers feel that they are not fighting for somebody else but for themselves and for the people. . . . Land has been allotted to all Red Army officers and men who are natives of the border area, but it is rather hard to allot land to those from distant areas. . . .

The average soldier needs six months' or a year's training before he can fight, but our soldiers, though recruited only yesterday, have to fight today with practically no training to speak of. Exceedingly poor in

military technique, they fight by courage alone. As a long period for rest and training is impossible, we shall see whether we can find ways to avoid certain battles in order to gain time for training. . . .

The Hunan Provincial Committee has asked us to attend to the material life of the soldiers and to make it at least a little better than that of the average worker or peasant. At present the very reverse is the case, for, besides rice, each man gets only five cents a day for cooking oil, salt, firewood and vegetables, and it is hard even to keep this up. The monthly cost of these items alone amounts to more than ten thousand silver dollars, which are obtained exclusively through expropriating the local bullies (bad landlords). We have now obtained cotton for the winter clothing of the whole army of five thousand men but are still short of cloth. Cold as the weather is, many of our men are still wearing two suits of clothes of single thickness. Fortunately we are inured to hardships. Furthermore all alike share the same hardships: everyone from the army commander down to the cook lives on a daily fare worth five cents, apart from grain. In the matter of pocket money, if two dimes are allotted, it is two dimes for everybody; if four dimes are allotted, it is four dimes for everybody. Thus the soldiers harbour no resentment against anyone. . . .

The officers do not beat the men; officers and men receive equal treatment, soldiers enjoy freedom of assembly and speech; cumbersome formalities and ceremonies are done away with; and the account books are open to inspection of all. The soldiers handle the messing arrangements. . . . All these measures are very satisfactory to the soldiers. The newly captured soldiers in particular feel that our army and the Kuomintang's army are worlds apart. They feel that, though in material life they are worse off in the Red Army than in the White Army, spiritually they are liberated. The fact that the same soldier who was not brave in the enemy army yesterday becomes very brave in the Red Army today shows precisely the impact of democracy. The Red Army is like a furnace in which all captured soldiers are melted down and transformed the moment they come over. . . .

From a report to the Central Committee of the Chinese Communist Party, 1928, entitled 'THE STRUGGLE IN THE CHINGKANG MOUNTAINS'

The significance of The Long March

It is a manifesto, an agitation corps and a seeding-machine. . . . It proclaims to the world that the Red Army is an army of heroes and that the imperialists and their jackals, Chiang Kai-shek and his like, are perfect nonentities. It announces the bankruptcy of the encirclement, pursuit, obstruction and interception attempted by the imperialists and Chiang Kai-shek. The Long March is also an agitation corps. It declares to the approximately two hundred million people of eleven provinces that only the road of the Red Army leads to their liberation. Without the Long March, how could the broad masses have known so quickly that there are such great ideas in the world as are upheld by the Red Army? The Long March is also a seeding-machine. It has sown many seeds in eleven provinces, which will sprout, grow leaves, blossom into flowers, bear fruit and yield a harvest in the future. . . .

. . . For twelve months we were under daily reconnaissance and bombing from the air by scores of planes; we were encircled, pursued, obstructed and intercepted on the ground by big forces of several hundred thousand men; we encountered untold difficulties and great obstacles on the way, but by keeping our two feet going we swept across a distance of more than twenty thousand li *through the length and breadth of eleven provinces. Has there ever been in history a long march like ours?*

The 'Three Chinas' 9

RIVALRY IN MANCHURIA

Under the Kuomintang Government, large numbers of Chinese had been persuaded to migrate into Manchuria, a Chinese province for three hundred years, a source of coal and iron, and a fertile grain-producing region. Japan, too, had vital interests in Manchuria, where she had built the South Manchurian Railway and held the lease of Port Arthur. Additionally, as part of the Twenty-one Demands, she had been given the right to own mines and iron and steel works in Manchuria, where, to protect her interests, she kept a puppet army financed from Japan.

During the summer of 1931, the Chinese and Japanese were several times in conflict in Manchuria. In one incident a Japanese army officer was killed by Chinese troops. Finally, there came the 'Mukden Incident'.

THE MUKDEN INCIDENT (1931)

During the evening of 18th September 1931, a bomb was exploded on the track of the South Manchurian Railway, just outside Mukden, an important city in Manchuria. The explosion was followed by the noise of gunfire—a sound of shots, so some historians say, that marked the real beginning of World War II.

The Japanese claimed that the Chinese had bombed the railway, whereupon Japanese troops had fired in defence of the line, and to drive off the Chinese saboteurs. In fact, the Japanese had contrived the whole affair as an excuse for mobilizing their troops and taking over Manchuria. Mukden and the other cities of South Manchuria passed, almost without resistance, into Japanese hands. This was the first stage in a conflict which was to last, with pauses, until 1945. At no time did the Japanese declare war on China. Had not Japan signed the Kellogg-Briand Pact which outlawed war?

JAPAN DEFIES THE LEAGUE OF NATIONS

On 21st September 1931, China appealed to the League of Nations for help. The League, at that time without the U.S.S.R. and the United States as member-nations, was timid and advised China and Japan to try and settle their quarrel peaceably. A commission of investigation, headed by Lord Lytton of Great Britain, was sent to study the situation on the spot. Meanwhile, the Japanese forces completed their conquest of Manchuria and a part of Inner Mongolia, joined both territories and created a new 'state' called Manchukuo.

The Lytton Report recommended that Manchuria should be restored to China. Japan then announced her resignation from the League. She had set an example of aggression and contempt for the League which was soon to be followed by Germany and Italy, and which paved the way for World War II. Even before leaving the League, however, Japan had struck yet another blow at China by the outright invasion of her territory.

THE SHANGHAI INCIDENT (1932)

After the invasion of Manchuria, the Chinese people refused to buy Japanese goods. The boycott was severe—and it began to hurt. Japanese businessmen in Shanghai appealed for help from their government. The 'help' arrived in January 1932, in the form of Japanese marines who were landed at Shanghai. After weeks of bitter fighting and heavy air-raids, the city fell to the Japanese, who claimed that their forces were there only to 'restore order'. They did not withdraw until the Chinese agreed to end the boycott.

The writing was now on the wall, however. Japan meant to dominate the Far East. She was enlarging her army and navy, and she was developing heavy industries in Manchukuo, an area that supplied her with coal, iron and petrol. She began to absorb parts of China south of the Great Wall. In May 1933, a Japanese army moved towards Peking. A truce was arranged and a demilitarized zone was declared between Peking and the Manchurian border. This zone was, in fact, a complete Japanese economic 'take-over'.

Chiang did nothing to resist this aggression. He was torn two ways. First and foremost, he was determined to destroy the 'enemy within'

—the Communist forces of Mao Tse-tung and other 'Red pockets of resistance' in various parts of China. He also needed time to build up the strength of his own forces for an all-out war with Japan. He knew this war *must* come. So, too, did Mao Tse-tung who was again building up the area under his rule in the Border Region.

THE BORDER REGION

Mao Tse-tung, as we know, had reached northern Shensi, one of the most remote and backward parts of China, with the survivors of the Long March. They lived in mud huts and in caves among the surrounding hills, and their only means of communication with the outside world was a pedal-operated radio transmitter.

Gradually, however, the Communists again built up their armies. Once more they went among the peasants, drove out the 'bad landlords', re-distributed the land, and set up village government. By the

(From left to right) Peng Teh-Huai, Vice Commander-in-Chief; Chu Teh, Commander-in-Chief; Yeh Chien-Ying, Chief of Staff; Nich Yung-Chen, Commander in Northern China; Chen Yi, Commander in Central China. This was the first time they had all been together in 10 years.

end of 1936, Mao was the ruler of nearly ten million people. In December of that year, the capital of the Chinese Soviet Republic was moved to the town of Yenan, which stood in a valley between hills that were honeycombed with caves, and these, for years were the homes and offices, the schools and hospitals and the air-raid shelters of the citizens and soldiers.

From Yenan, in 1936, Mao Tse-tung twice appealed to Chiang Kai-shek to form a united front against the Japanese, whose army in Manchukuo was preparing to come over the border.

Chiang would have none of this. Instead, he called upon his troops to destroy the 'red bandits'. He ordered the Manchurian armies, under the command of 'The Young Marshal', Chang Hsëuh-liang, which had been driven out of their country by the Japanese, to attack the Red base. It was a mistake. The Manchurians had no real quarrel with the Communists. What they wanted was an anti-Japanese war to free their homeland. Chiang then flew to Sian, in southern Shensi, to order an all-out attack on the Communist stronghold. His arrival there led to yet another 'incident'.

THE SIAN INCIDENT

Chiang threatened to dismiss the Young Marshal and to call in loyal troops to disarm the Manchurian soldiers. The Marshal, in his turn, talked with his officers. They decided to mutiny. A division of their troops overpowered Chiang's bodyguard: the General was arrested. The Communists were informed of his arrest, and sent Chou En-lai, for whose capture Chiang had offered an 80,000 dollar reward, to negotiate with the prisoner. In the end, Chiang reluctantly agreed to call off the war against the Communists, and to form a united front against the Japanese. The Red Army would be renamed the Eighth Route Army, with Chiang as overall commander, and the Communists would disband the Soviet Republic. When this agreement was reached, Chiang was permitted to leave Sian alive.

The truce was a turning-point in Chinese affairs. The Communists had won a great deal—notably a breathing-space in which to increase their power. In a short space of time the Soviet area covered nearly a hundred thousand square miles; the Kuomintang blockade was lifted and supplies and equipment flowed into the Border Region. For once, the Chinese nation was united for war.

THE CHINA 'INCIDENT'

The long-awaited conflict began in July 1937. There was no declaration of war; in Japan, in fact, it was called 'The China Incident'.

On the night of 7th July 1937, Chinese soldiers clashed with a Japanese force at the Marco Polo Bridge, near Peking—a place where the Japanese had no right to be. The Japanese armies in Manchukuo at once marched south. In Shensi their advance was fiercely resisted and brought to a halt by the Communist Eighth Route Army. Elsewhere, the Japanese advance was swift and unfailing. In August, Shanghai was attacked and became the scene of bitter fighting, in which Chiang's army was hard hit. Nanking fell in December 1937; Hankow and Canton were lost in October 1938. Chiang moved his capital to Chungking, above the deep gorges of the Yangtze.

In the north-west, the Red capital of Yenan was pounded from the air. Its people, for the most part, lived and conducted their affairs in a bomb-proof cave-city dug out of the high cliffs on each side of their valley. While Chiang's forces suffered defeat after defeat, Communist power and prestige grew steadily. The Red Army fought the Japanese in the way it had waged war for years, its guerilla-units appearing unexpectedly in the heart of enemy territory, cutting off supplies, striking at weak points, destroying mines and railways, then retreating into the forests and the mountains where tanks and big guns were of little use against them.

By the end of 1939, there were 'three' Chinas. In the east, there was Occupied China, where the Japanese had control of the most important cities and the seaboard provinces. In the south-west, was Kuomintang China, where Chiang had an uncertain hold on several provinces, but could not win back any lost territory. In the north-west was Red China, its forces putting up a brave and stubborn resistance, winning new territory by guerilla-warfare, and the hearts and minds of the peasant-masses by their programme of land-reform. By the end of 1940, they had 'liberated' and were in control of 150 counties, with a population of 100,000,000 people.

Chiang saw the danger of this, and re-opened the civil war, ordering a blockade and new offensives against the Border Region. They met with little success. The war in China now reached a stalemate. The Japanese made few further gains of territory.

The outbreak of war in Europe, in September 1939, gave the Japanese militarists the chance for which they had waited. In

September 1940, Japan made an alliance, the Rome-Berlin-Tokyo-Axis, with Hitler and Mussolini. Just over a year later, having decided that Russia was already beaten by the Germans, she entered upon the Pacific War.

THE PACIFIC WAR (1941-5)

On 7th December 1941, without any declaration of war, planes from a Japanese carrier fleet attacked the United States navy base at Pearl Harbour, Hawaii. In this way, the Japanese came into World War II—and ensured that the United States should do the same.

To begin with, the Japanese had things all their own way. In a matter of months they took Burma, Thailand and Malaya. They overran the islands of the South Pacific, the East Indies, the Philippines and the Gilbert Islands. They made landings on New Guinea and the Solomons; they advanced overland and threatened to pour into India.

China meanwhile had become an ally of Great Britain and the United States. Chiang's government, the one recognized by the Allies, was supplied with money, arms and munitions, but made little effort to take the offensive against the Japanese. Chiang, in fact, was storing up supplies for the fight with the Communists 'when the time came'.

The second half of 1942 saw the tide begin to turn against the Japanese. By 1943 the Allies were taking the offensive in the Pacific War, fighting battle after battle on land, sea, and in the air. A year later, the Americans held the superiority in aircraft-carriers and planes. It grew plain that the Japanese must be defeated in the end. By early 1945, the Allies had won islands that brought Japan itself within range of heavy bombers; her cities and industries were pounded from the air, and her fleet, to all useful purpose, had ceased to exist. The Japanese, however, seemed determined to fight to the death. Their resistance grew more and more desperate as the steel net tightened around them, and the Allied forces grew closer to the four islands.

By then the Allies were in possession of the most frightful weapon ever devised by the mind of man. They issued an ultimatum: unless Japan surrendered she would be struck a terrible blow. The Japanese Government refused to surrender.

Early in August 1945, atom bombs were dropped on Hiroshima

General and Madame Chiang Kai-shek in Chungking at a tea party given to 60 WAACs

and Nagasaki. On the day that Nagasaki was smashed and scorched and blasted, the Soviet Union declared war on Japan. Her armies swept into Manchuria, where they met with little resistance. On 14th August the Emperor of Japan announced his country's surrender. The Pacific War was at an end.

THE FINAL STRUGGLE (1947-9)

In the last four months of 1945, the United States gave great help to Chiang Kai-shek by transporting hundreds of thousands of Kuomintang troops to east and north China, where they took control of Peking and Tientsin. With Russian permission, 1500 Kuomintang troops were flown daily to Manchuria to take over from the Soviet forces there. Mao's Yenan radio protested violently against the American aid given to Chiang, claiming that the arms supplied to him would soon be turned against the Communists.

For a spell, in 1946, there was an uneasy peace in China. A special envoy, General George C. Marshall, was sent from America to try and arrange some form of peaceful settlement between the two sides. A cease-fire agreement was signed; conferences and peace-talks were held. During this time of truce, Kuomintang troops occupied further cities, while the Communists enlarged their territories. Finally each side accused the other of violating the truce. In July 1946, Chiang's pilots, flying American aeroplanes, raided Yenan. The peace was over. Once again the armies of China's two strong-men flung themselves at each other.

Chiang's forces were well-trained and equipped, but proved no match for the Red armies, which now had the support of the people. The Communists offered order and safety, reform and recovery, instead of the want and misery and corruption that the people had known under Kuomintang rule. Above all, they offered 'the land to the peasants'.

The Red Armies swept across the face of China to win victory after victory at breathless pace. In the south, whole Kuomintang armies surrendered and went over to the Communists who now fought with vast quantities of captured American equipment. By the end of 1948, their soldiers were three million in number. The provincial cities fell to them, one after another. By early 1949, they had taken the main industrial and commercial cities of North China. Shanghai surrendered after little struggle, and on its buildings there appeared portraits of Mao Tse-tung five storeys high.

On 31st January, the 200,000 defenders of Peking gave up without a struggle. On 3rd February, 1949, the Red troops entered the city, column after column armed with weapons of Japanese or American make—infantry, tanks, armoured trucks and heavy artillery.

It was the end of Kuomintang rule. On 1st October 1949, Mao Tse-tung proclaimed the establishment of the People's Republic of China, and told the vast multitude gathered to hear him: 'The Chinese nation will never be insulted again. We have stood up! Let the world tremble!'

Documentary Nine

From a telegram sent by Mao Tse-tung to Chiang Kai-shek's government in Nanking, May 1936, appealing for a united front against the Japanese

---

The Revolutionary Military Committee of the Red Army hereby solemnly advises the gentlemen of the Nanking government that at this critical moment of the threat of immediate destruction to the nation and the people, you ought, in all reason, to break with your past and, in the spirit of the maxim, 'Brothers quarrelling at home will join forces against attacks from the outside', to stop the nation-wide civil war. . . . This will not only be for your own good, but also a blessing to the nation and the country. If, however, you obstinately refuse to awaken to reason and want to become collaborators and traitors, then your rule will certainly collapse in the end, and you will certainly be spurned and overthrown by the people of the whole country. The old saying has it, 'Pointed at by a thousand accusing fingers, one dies even though in perfect health'. And again, 'The butcher becomes a Buddha the moment he drops his cleaver'. These are words for you gentlemen to digest and ponder.

From SELECTED WORKS of Mao Tse-Tung

From a speech made by Mao Tse-tung to the Central Committee of the Chinese Communist Party, 1938.

As a national war of resistance is going on, we must further contend for military power for the nation. . . . Every Communist must grasp the truth: 'Political power grows out of the barrel of a gun.' Our principle is that the Party commands the gun, and the gun will never be allowed to command the Party. But it is also true that with guns at our disposal we can really build up the Party organization and the Eighth Route Army has built up a powerful Party organization in North China. We can also rear cadres and create schools, culture and mass movements. Everything in Yenan has been built up by means of the gun. Anything can grow out of the barrel of a gun. According to the Marxist theory of the state, the army is the chief component of the political power of a state. Whoever wants to seize the political power of the state and to maintain it must have a strong army. . . . Experience in the class-struggle of the era of imperialism teaches us that the working class and the toiling masses cannot defeat the armed bourgeois and landlords except by the power of the gun; in this sense we can even say that the whole world can be remoulded only with the gun.

From SELECTED WORKS, Mao Tse-tung

Extract from a report by John P. Davies,
of the U.S. Department of State, 1944.

Only if he is able to enlist foreign intervention on a scale equal to the Japanese invasion of China will Chiang probably be able to crush the Communists. But foreign intervention on such a scale would seem to be unlikely. Relying upon his dispirited shambling legions, his decadent corrupt bureaucracy, his sterile political moralisms and such nervous foreign support as he can muster, the Generalissimo may nevertheless plunge China into civil war. He cannot succeed, however, where the Japanese in more than seven years of determined striving have failed. The Communists are already too strong for him.

If the Generalissimo neither precipitates a civil war nor reaches an understanding with the Communists, he is still confronted with defeat. Chiang's feudal China can not long coexist alongside a modern dynamic popular government in North China.

The Communists are in China to stay. And China's destiny is not Chiang's but theirs.

From UNITED STATES RELATIONS WITH CHINA
WITH SPECIAL REFERENCE TO THE PERIOD 1944-9

10

LIMITED CAPITALISM

By the end of 1949, the Red Army held all of the Chinese mainland; the People's Government had been proclaimed; and Chiang Kai-shek had fled, with such troops as remained loyal to him, to the island of Formosa (also called Taiwan).

The task that faced the new Central People's Government Council, with Mao Tse-tung as its chairman, was a formidable one: China had not known effective government for nearly half a century; it was pitifully backward in industrial development; food was in short supply, the economy was shattered and no help was forthcoming from the Western powers, who looked upon the Communist regime with suspicion and distrust.

A cotton mill in Shanghai

Mao's thoughts and portrait are brought to the people in Hsich Chen province, by the People's Liberation Army

So, too, did many Chinese 'capitalists'—financiers, businessmen, landowners—who dreaded a Communist 'take-over' of their properties. These were the traditional class-enemies of Communism, who might join with unfriendly powers to stage a counter-revolution. In view of China's present backwardness, however, Ch'en Yün, Minister of Heavy Industry, stated that, for the moment, it would be 'beneficial to the country and the people for the national capitalists to develop industry and make investments in it for a long time'.

While, for the moment, the new government was prepared to permit 'limited capitalism', it seized control of heavy industries and big commercial establishments, closed down private banks and replaced them with a State Bank which could finance schemes approved by the leadership. The new state trading companies bought and sold goods at a fixed rate to help call a halt to inflation.

THOUGHT REFORM

The Communist Government recognized that there were many people who had no true sympathy with their regime—artists and writers, scientists, scholars and teachers, who had come under foreign influences and who must be 're-educated' through 'thought reform' and the 'remoulding of individuals'. Over the next few years the whole of China was to be subjected to mass persuasion through meetings, rallies, newspaper articles, radio and big character posters. Communist Party officials were to move into villages, factories, schools and universities, into every street in every town, to lecture and persuade, threaten or denounce, those who were 'against the government'. Compulsory courses in Marxism were introduced into schools and universities; people of all ages were pressed into taking part in processions and parades; newspapers and books were brought under government control so that it became impossible to read criticisms of the Communist regime.

'Whoever wants to oppose Communism,' warned Mao Tse-tung, 'must prepare to be smashed to pieces.' In July 1950, the death sentence was decreed for the leaders of gangs 'who take up arms against the people's government'. By a law of 21st February 1951, spying and engagement in counter-revolutionary activities were made punishable by imprisonment or death. Even so, the Communist leadership preferred, when dealing with enemies, 'to allow them to live and remould themselves through labour into new people'.

FIVE YEAR PLANS

The chief concern of the new regime was to make China into a modern industrial state. This was to be done by a programme which closely followed the steps taken by Soviet Russia from 1918 onwards: through a series of 'Five Year Plans' by which the government would control the development of industry, by great production-drives, and by harnessing the 'work-power' of the Chinese people.

The immediate aim was to boost China's agricultural production so that a surplus might be sold abroad and the profit used to buy machinery and equipment for the expansion of industry. The first step was to reform the system of land-holding.

LAND REFORM

The Communists, who do not believe in the private ownership of land, had already begun to give 'land to the tiller' in those parts of China which they had 'liberated' before 1949. Under a 1950 Agrarian Reform Law, this process was now put into operation all over China. It was meant to do more than relieve the poverty of the peasants, however; it served, also, as a means of 'eliminating' those landowners who might be dangerous opponents of the new order.

Thousands of *cadres*, or groups of Communist Party officials, were sent into the countryside to organize the peasants into Village Associations, and to urge that the land, implements, surplus grain and draught animals of the landlords should be confiscated and distributed to poor peasants with little or no land.

During village 'accusation meetings' the cadres encouraged the peasants to denounce 'bad landlords' who had ill-used them in the past. If these landlords were held to be 'class enemies' they were tried by special People's Tribunals which had the right to sentence 'criminal landlords' to imprisonment or death. Death sentences could be carried out on the spot. Statistics are not available but it is believed that not less than one million people were put to death during the time of these purges. Many others were put into forced labour camps for 're-education', while those of better repute were given an equal share of confiscated property and the chance to 'reform themselves through labour'. Land reform was completed within two years, and did much to strengthen the grip of the Communist Government on the rural population. In 1951-2 the People's Tribunals were also active in the cities in campaigns waged against 'lawbreaking merchants', corruption in government officials, and businessmen and industrialists who were held to be guilty of tax-evasion.

MUTUAL-AID TEAMS

Redistribution of land was meant only as a first step in a much wider programme of reform, aimed at the eventual state control of agriculture. The Communists knew that small-scale farming would not supply the food for China's growing population, or provide a surplus for export. Large-scale mechanized farming, using scientific methods, was needed. The peasants had to be 'educated' to this view gradually.

Machaio Commune
The women help to cultivate the land

In 1952, the cadres began to encourage the villagers to join together in 'mutual-aid teams', usually made up of about ten families. The farmers kept their own land, but pooled labour and equipment, particularly for harvesting and sowing. Expensive agricultural machinery could be bought for the use of the team as a whole, with each member paying a share according to the size of his holding. By August 1952, it was estimated that thirty-five million peasant families had been organized into ten million teams.

THE CO-OPERATIVES

At the end of 1953, the villagers were urged to consider the value of 'co-operative farming': that is, for a large number of them to pool their land in one big tract, which could be devoted to one crop, and which might be worked jointly and with much greater profit.

Under this system several mutual-aid teams were joined together; the members pooled land, animals and machinery, and carried out sowing and harvesting as a joint operation. They still owned their land, but a committee—under the guidance of a cadre—decided which crop to raise and was responsible for its marketing. When the crop was sold, a government tax was paid and a sum set aside for the needs of the following season. Profits were shared among members according to the contribution they had made in land, equipment, and hours of work.

This movement towards large-scale farming met with some opposition from the peasants. In some districts, they slaughtered their livestock rather than hand them over for the common good.

In 1955, however, Mao Tse-tung ordered a new propaganda drive. By 1957, he said, half of the peasants must be organized into collective farming; by 1960, all of them. The cadres set to work with such vigour that hundreds of millions of peasants were convinced that the well-being of Chinese agriculture, and her future industrialization, depended upon co-operative farming and the change-over from private ownership to common ownership. So successful was this campaign that, by February 1957, more than 96 per cent of the peasants were in the co-operatives.

Meanwhile, the leadership had forged ahead with the programme for industrial development.

THE 'GREAT LEAP'

The First Five Year Plan (1953-7) called upon the Chinese people to concentrate their energies on the production of food, coal, iron and steel, and to produce only a minimum of 'consumer goods': pots and pans, furniture, clothing, etc., which do not help in the making of other goods. The workers were told that they must dedicate their labour to the *future* welfare of their country.

The period of the first Five Year Plan saw a remarkable growth in industry, particularly in heavy industry. By 1957, China was in a position to manufacture cars, lorries and tractors, oil tankers and cargo ships, light aircraft, hydro-electric stations and steel works.

This success led Mao Tse-tung, in 1958, to call upon the Chinese people to make a 'great leap forward'—to 'build up work enthusiasm, work bitterly hard for three years and promote industry and agriculture'. The 'Great Leap', in fact, was meant to change China almost overnight into a self-supporting, modern industrial state.

Workers at an iron and steel plant in Northern China

The new 'high-pressure drive' seemed to lead, at first, to great achievements. The efforts and enthusiasm of the people were astonishing. Millions of peasants, who were largely idle between harvest and sowing, were set to work laying roads and railways, building dikes, digging canals and irrigation trenches. High targets were set for miners, steel-workers, mill-workers and peasant farmers.

Girls on a commune in Southern China use an electric husker to strip rice off the stalks. Dry stalks are used for fuel or thatching

1958 was a tremendous year for China. She reaped a record harvest, the production of food grain increasing from 200 million tons to 250 million tons. The peasants were filled with an immense enthusiasm for the task in hand, and somewhat carried away by it. Everyone turned to making steel in thousands of 'backyard furnaces'—though the steel turned out was inferior in quality. Men and machines, and often the land itself, were worked to such a point that exhaustion set in. Projects were set in being and workers were moved about in great numbers, sacrificing their personal freedoms for the good of the nation. A by-product of all this activity was the appearance of the Communes.

Two girls from a commune production team make simple hoes
The communes are supposed to be self-sufficient

THE COMMUNES

In April 1958 in the province of Honan, twenty-seven agricultural co-operatives joined themselves together to form the Weihsing (Sputnik) Enlarged Co-operative, which had a population of more than forty thousand people. The idea met with immediate Government approval, and Mao Tse-tung, who was reported to have given the name 'Commune' to the new organization, made a tour of North China to advocate and further the scheme. The movement spread with an almost incredible speed. By November 1958, it was stated

A commune doctor examines a patient
Every commune has a health station and sometimes a small hospital
Efforts are being made to attract doctors from the cities to the country

that 99 per cent of the peasantry had merged their co-operatives into 26,000 Communes.

Their advantage, as Mao pointed out, lay in the fact that they controlled not only farming, but many other useful things as well. They set up small industries to provide work for their members during the time when there was no demand for agricultural labour; they provided schools, welfare and medical services, and homes for the aged; they undertook building projects and water-storage schemes, provided canteens for workers' meals, and nurseries for small children—which set housewives free for work in field or factory. Also, under the party cadres, the Communes made it easy for the central government to plan and direct the activities of the people.

Difficulties were experienced in establishing Communes but there can be little doubt that they have had a powerful effect on Chinese society. As the basic unit of government in the countryside, they provide the peasants with amenities and welfare services, and have helped to solve the problem of agricultural under-employment.

DROUGHT AND FLOOD (1959-61)

Disastrous weather in 1959-61 brought three calamitous harvests, droughts and floods causing the loss of crops throughout a large part of the country. Food production fell back to the level of 1956. In 1961, to avoid famine, China had to go abroad for its food, and bought ten million tons of grain from Canada, Australia and South America. Food was rationed, but shared out in a way that was fair and ensured no hoarding.

The food shortage was a severe set-back to the economy. It was also discovered that the 'Great Leap' had not succeeded. Production, generally, had fallen far below the wildly-optimistic targets set by the planners. When the crisis was over, the Chinese people were urged to tighten their belts and work even harder to achieve equality with the big industrial nations of the world.

CHINA'S INDUSTRIAL REVOLUTION

There can be no doubt that, since the Communist take-over, China has gone a long way to becoming an industrial power. Her people were set the task of trying to make good in twenty years what it took the British people two hundred years to achieve. Already, great strides have been made in heavy industry, particularly steel production. Though China lacks the vast natural resources of the United States or Soviet Russia, she has large oil reserves and rich deposits of coal and iron ore, along with adequate supplies of those metals and minerals required by modern industry, all discovered by a proper scientific investigation of the country's natural resources undertaken since 1949.

A sign of the scientific and technological progress made was China's entry into the dangerous world of nuclear explosions when she tested her first A-bomb in October 1964. That she should feel called upon to make such warlike demonstrations has been largely due to her continuing distrust of the nations of the West.

THE POLICY OF CONTAINMENT

Immediately following World War II many of the nations of the world split up into two hostile groups: on one hand the Communist countries, led by the Soviet Union and on the other, the democratic countries, led by the United States. America took on the task of stopping the spread of Communism in any part of the world by following a policy of 'containment'; that is, by giving all possible help to those backward countries where Communism was likely to succeed, and by offering military assistance to any country faced by Communist 'aggression'. This policy led the Americans, who were filled with alarm at the thought of Communist China closely-allied with Soviet Russia, to offer arms and assistance to Chiang Kai-shek's Kuomintang government in an effort to halt the advance of Communism. This, in its turn, has created the problem of Taiwan and the 'two Chinas'.

TAIWAN (FORMOSA)

When Chiang Kai-shek moved to Taiwan in 1949, the United States persisted in the view that his was still the 'lawful' Government of China, and continued to supply him with arms and equipment. He was thus able to fortify his positions on Taiwan—an island of some

Quemoy Island
A Nationalist soldier stands guard against the People's Republic

ten million people—and on the neighbouring islands of Quemoy and Matsu. Taiwan has become a kind of 'little China', still under Nationalist rule.

In 1957, and again in 1958, the People's Government threatened to attack and 'liberate' the Kuomintang-ruled islands. The U.S. promptly moved military forces into the area and announced that they might be used to defend the islands, which had been shelled and bombarded from the mainland.

American hostility to the People's Republic, and continued support for Chiang Kai-shek, poisoned relations between the two countries throughout the fifties and sixties. The early 1970's, however, have seen a spectacular change in the American attitude to China.

CHINA ADMITTED TO U.N. (Oct. 25, 1971)

For more than twenty years, the U.S.A. refused to recognize the People's Government and blocked its admission to the United Nations. Washington, it would seem, has now realized that the U.S. must accept the 'reality' of the People's Republic and the inescapable fact that China's cooperation is essential in the establishment of any sort of world order.

On October 25, 1971, the U.N. General Assembly adopted a resolution to admit the People's Republic of China to membership of the United Nations, including a permanent seat on the Security Council, and at the same time to expel 'forthwith' the Chinese Nationalist regime on Taiwan. This event was followed by further friendly overtures made by America to Communist China.

'A WEEK THAT CHANGED THE WORLD'

On February 21, 1972, President Nixon of the United States, his wife, and a party of high-ranking officials, flew to Peking. The American party was welcomed by Mr. Chou En-lai, Prime Minister of the People's Republic, and President Nixon was later received by Chairman Mao in his own residence. There followed a week of conducted tours, official receptions, and high-level talks in what was described as 'an atmosphere of great cordiality'.

The world learned, from an official statement, that the United States had agreed to 'withdraw its forces and military installations on Taiwan as the tension in the area diminishes'; and had undertaken to send a senior representative of the United States to Peking from time to time for 'consultations to further the normalization of relations between the two countries'.

At a farewell-banquet President Nixon said that his seven-day visit had marked 'a week that changed the world'. It may certainly be regarded as a tacit, if not open, recognition by the United States of the People's Republic of China.

THE WAR IN KOREA (1950-51)

At the end of the Pacific War in 1945, there were Japanese troops in Korea. It was agreed that the Russians should accept their surrender in North Korea, and the Americans in the south. For the sake of convenience, a 'boundary' was fixed at the 38th parallel of latitude,

The Allies agreed that Korea should be independent. Finally, however, two governments were set up—one, after an election, in the American zone; the other, the People's Republic of North Korea, a Communist Government, in the Soviet zone. The two big powers then withdrew their occupation forces.

In June 1950, the North Korean army swept over the border in an attempt to invade and seize the South. The United Nations declared that North Korea was an 'aggressor' and called upon member-nations to supply troops to aid the South. Sixteen nations sent troops and equipment, but the brunt of the war was borne by the United States. The American General, Douglas MacArthur, was given command of the United Nations Army.

This army forced its way into North Korea in a drive towards the Yalu River, the boundary between Korea and Manchuria. China then sent several hundred thousand 'volunteer' troops into Korea to prevent an American victory. There followed long months of bitter fighting. The war ended in the armistice of 27th July 1953. The 'two Koreas' continue to exist, but with much the same boundaries.

The policy of China in seeking 'spheres of influence' in those countries on her borders, with the aim of securing her frontiers, and of trying to gain her ends by indirect war and subversion, led to her involvement in a longer and more bitter war in Vietnam.

THE WAR IN VIETNAM (INDO-CHINA)

Vietnam is one of the three states in what was called Indo-China: the other two are Laos and Cambodia. In 1883, during the European scramble for colonies, the French took and held Indo-China until its occupation by the Japanese in World War II. After the Japanese surrender, in 1945, the Indo-Chinese Communist Party, led by Ho Chi Minh, organized a national front, the Vietminh, which took over Vietnam. He let French troops remain after France had promised Vietnam a large degree of self-government. Fighting broke out between the Vietminh and the French forces, however, and in December 1946, there began a war which lasted nearly eight years. The fighting was largely guerilla warfare, waged in the jungle, and the Chinese Communists helped the Vietminh with arms and training.

In 1954, the French sued for peace. A conference of France, Great Britain, the United States, Soviet Russia and Communist China met at Geneva to settle the problem. As a consequence, Vietnam was divided at the 17th parallel. The Communists (the Vietminh, that is) took the northern half; and the southern half became an independent republic. Both sides were supposed to be free of foreign troops, but America—wishing to stop the spread of Communism in Asia—began to give increasing military and financial aid to South Vietnam, while Russia and China financed the North.

Within a few years, Communist guerilla-fighters in South Vietnam began a struggle to 'liberate the South'. In 1960, North Vietnam openly declared its support for these 'Vietcong', and has since supplied them with men and arms. The United States replied, in the first place, by sending military advisers to South Vietnam. Then, in October 1964, as the war grew 'hotter' and a Communist victory, backed by China, seemed likely, she took the step of sending in fighting-men, ships, and aircraft. In December 1965, there were more than 180,000 troops in Vietnam, but over the next four years, American aid 'escalated'. Despite gradual withdrawal of some forces with a view to increasing the Vietnamization of the Southern armies and encouraging negotiations for a settlement, the war goes on. In talks in Saigon in July, 1969 President Nixon said, 'let us with determination and goodwill seek to put an end to the destruction and suffering which the people of Vietnam, North and South, have borne so long'.

THE QUARREL WITH RUSSIA

Events in recent years have not borne out the American fear of a Russian-Chinese alliance. The two Communist giants have, in fact, quarrelled and now look upon each other with suspicion; for ten years, relations between the two countries have been as bad as international relations can be, short of going to war. There have been a number of clashes between Russians and Chinese along the immense frontier that separates the two countries—a frontier that has been called '7000 miles of distrust, intrigue and jealous rivalry'. In March 1969, frontier guards of both sides were killed in clashes on Damansky island, on the fringe of the Manchurian Plain, and both countries launched bitter attacks upon each other through press and radio.

It should be remembered that, during the years of Mao's struggle with the Kuomintang, he had received little help from Soviet Russia. He had, in fact, been looked upon with some suspicion by the Russian leaders of the day, since his policy of giving up all thought of city-risings and his organizing of the peasant masses was, in Soviet eyes, a departure from Communist doctrine. In recent years, these two great nations have quarrelled over the form that each thinks Communism should take in the 20th century world.

The Chinese have accused the Soviet leaders of being 'modern revisionists': of turning away from the ideas and theories of Karl Marx and betraying the Communist cause by holding out the hand of friendship to the Capitalist countries of the West. Soviet foreign policy in recent years has, in fact, been one of 'peaceful coexistence of States with different social systems': the belief that the Capitalist countries and the Communist may live side by side in peace. Mao Tse-tung will have none of this. He still sees Britain and America as 'imperialist powers', the eternal enemies against whom all true Communists must struggle until they are finally overthrown. It is his aim to make China leader of the world Communist movement; to give every possible help to revolutionary wars in order to hasten the end of Capitalism throughout the world.

A STRUGGLE FOR POWER INSIDE CHINA

After the failure of the 'Great Leap' it became clear that there was a difference of opinion between the 'thought' of Mao Tse-tung and that of other 'top men' of the Chinese Communist Party. Even after 1949, Mao had remained a revolutionary at heart, one who saw life as a kind of never-ending guerilla warfare. To him, the Communist triumph over the Kuomintang did not mean that the revolution was at an end, but that a new struggle had begun; a struggle to turn all of China into a classless society in which all the people lived in self-contained collectives and had the power to vote the necessary officials and administrators in and out of office.

In the years after 1949, however, there had risen in China a new 'upper crust' of intellectuals and officials who had ideas of their own and who felt no need to live at the same level as the peasants in order to play their part in Mao's ideal society. They were ready to allow class divisions and permit capitalist methods among the people if it suited the needs of the moment.

In 1959 Mao was replaced as Chairman of the Republic by Liu Shao-chi, but remained Chairman of the Party's central committee and politburo (chief policy-making body). For a time his influence seemed at a low ebb. Meanwhile, the peasants were allowed to raise vegetables and livestock on private plots of land and to sell them in 'free' markets.

Mao then emerged from the background and began a 'Culture

Liu Shao-chi

Lin Piao

Revolution' to educate the Chinese millions round to his way of thinking. The young people were urged to model themselves on Mao himself. To this end, millions of copies of the 'Little Red Book' containing the 'Thoughts' of Mao were distributed among the population to be looked on as a kind of 'Bible', and millions of youthful 'Red Guards' were organized to attack in one way or another the enemies of Mao's policies.

At the end of September 1965, Marshal Lin Piao, the Minister of Defence and Red Army Chief, made a fierce declaration in support of Mao's ideas and the two appeared to have gone into partnership against those who did not see eye-to-eye with them.

In January 1967, Lin Piao was reported to have described China as being 'in a state of civil war'. There were newspaper accounts of violence in Chinese cities; of street fighting between workers and Red Guards; of riots among the peasants, and strikes and disturbances among railwaymen and industrial workers.

The outcome of these events appeared to be a victory for Mao and Lin Piao, who together dominated the Ninth Congress of the Chinese Communist Party, which opened in April 1969, when Lin was officially named as Mao's successor. Then followed a period of mystery and uncertainty. For a long spell Lin simply disappeared from the Chinese scene; there was no mention of his name in press and radio communiqués and he was no longer seen at public functions.

During the early months of 1972, there were reports in British newspapers that Lin had attempted to seize power in China by assassinating Mao, had failed, and then died in an air-crash while making a dash for freedom.

Lurid as these accounts were, they were given official confirmation by Chinese spokesmen in July 1972, in statements made in Peking, Algiers, Paris and London, acknowledging that Lin Piao had died on September 12, 1971, after plotting to 'usurp the leadership of the party, the Government, and the Army'. Having failed in an attempt to assassinate Mao Tse-tung, it seems that he fled by aeroplane towards the Soviet Union. His plane, however, crashed

Youthful Red Guards march through Peking
They carry copies of Mao's 'Little Red Book' and his portrait

for some unknown reason in Mongolia, 100 miles outside Chinese airspace. Only Lin, his wife and son, and a handful of accomplices were in the aircraft.

The Soviet authorities, who received the bodies of the dead Chinese from their Mongolian allies after the crash, have expressed concern that the Chinese are trying to link Lin Piao with the Soviet Union in an effort to discredit Moscow by suggesting that the Russians were involved in the plot to overthrow Mao.

With the passing of Lin, it is possible that China may turn to a collective leadership, with Chou En-lai holding second place after Mao Tse-tung. To date, the ageing Mao has kept his grip on the reins of power by retaining his leadership of the Party. Certainly, his influence as a Thinker and Teacher is felt throughout the Communist movement. Mao, it must be remembered, is more than an elder statesman: he is also a Communist 'theorist'. He adapted the

teachings of Marx and Lenin to Chinese conditions and created an Asiatic form of Marxism. His 'thoughts' and writings have given Communism a new direction, and a sense of purpose and dedication to the largest population ever to live under one government.

GENERAL EFFECTS OF THE CHINESE REVOLUTION

Are the Chinese people better off than they used to be? There is no easy answer to that question; it will not emerge from a study of statistics for the production of steel, or from a reading of *Quotations From Chairman Mao Tse-tung*. Nor may one sensibly compare the purposeful, well-ordered China of today with the chaotic, war-torn China at the time of the Kuomintang and the Japanese invasion.

Most of us in the West are likely to seek an answer in terms of 'freedom of speech' and 'democratic government' as opposed to the 'Party line' and 'Communist dictatorship'. We are told that the poorest Chinese no longer die of hunger, but that they have been forced to surrender their freedom. China is not a democracy but a 'totalitarian' state. Her leaders make all the decisions of any importance. Everyone is expected to do as they say. To ensure that they do there is a political secret service within the country, which has its own armed military force for the suppression of revolt. It is responsible for the supervision of every Chinese household and for the running of concentration and labour camps which are reported to hold some ten million prisoners.

The great masses of the Chinese people, however, know little about democracy, or the political and social freedoms which we take for granted. Under the rule of the Emperors, the Chinese peasant had nothing of freedom, and was often left to die of disease and starvation. His Government, today, rules over him with a strong hand, demands that he works hard, forces him to pay taxes and obey the law—but, in return, it sees that he has food and work and a measure of social security. Moreover, he is aware of his country's growing strength, and has a feeling of pride in the part he is called upon to play.

Whereas, in the Old China, education was the privilege of a few, the modern Communist state spends large sums of money on schools of all types. A simplified way of reading and writing the old Chinese characters has been taught to millions of people who were once

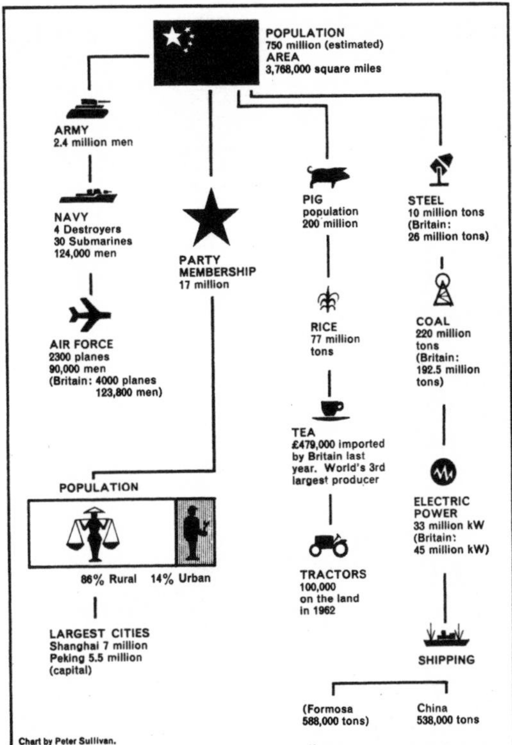

China: Facts and Figures

illiterate. Women are no longer considered inferior creatures, but have been given equality with men. The health of the nation has been greatly improved; disease is being controlled; doctors are being trained in their thousands; hospitals are being built. Many scientists and engineers are graduating from newly-established universities. China is in the process of becoming a great industrial nation, and may one day match the industrial strength of Russia and America.

THE PLACE OF COMMUNISM IN THE EVOLUTION OF THE CHINESE PEOPLE

To many foreign observers the present Communist regime in China appears to bear a strong likeness to the Manchu Empire of the past. What has happened in China, it is said, is entirely in keeping with the

natural evolution of the Chinese people. The Communist movement, for example, did nothing more than give leadership and purpose to a peasant revolution—similar to the Taiping Rebellion—which was, in any case, bound to happen when the old Empire collapsed. In recent years, also, China has again isolated herself behind a 'bamboo curtain', and has become a self-contained, continuing civilization in which the Communists have destroyed all Western influences. As in the past, there are 'barbarians', that is the non-Communists, living beyond China's borders, but they will, in time, be 'civilized', just as the Chinese civilized the barbarians of old. For centuries the Chinese people lived according to the teachings of Confucius, by a system of rules that directed their daily behaviour. Have they not, today, substituted the teachings of Marx and Mao Tse-tung? The history of China is a story of the rise and fall of governments: when a dynasty had passed its peak and there came a period of confusion and disorder, it was overthrown and a new order was established. Instead of a Manchu Empire there is, today, a Marxist Empire, ruled over by a select body of men who are the Communist 'mandarins' of the 20th century. The wheel of history, in short, has turned full circle; and Communist China is a 'more up-to-date, more ruthless, more efficient version of what the Celestial Empire had been for thousands of years'.

There was a time when the Chinese people had much to give the world, and there was a 'one-way traffic' in ideas from China to Europe. China led the world and achieved a great civilization. In recent years, she has progressed and gained in power. She is the most populous nation on the face of the earth; a nation that we must respect—and expect to play a leading part in world affairs.

A Shanghai Street

Documentary Ten

Extracts from the LITTLE RED BOOK of Mao Tse-tung

Section 2. Classes and Class Struggle.

The ruthless economic exploitation and political oppression of the peasants by the landlord class forced them into numerous uprisings against its rule. . . . It was the class struggles of the peasants, the peasant uprisings and peasant wars that constituted the real motive force of historical development in Chinese feudal society.

It is up to us to organize the people. As for the reactionaries in China, it is up to us to organize the people to overthrow them. Everything reactionary is the same; if you don't hit it, it won't fall. This is also like sweeping the floor; as a rule, where the broom does not reach, the dust will not vanish of itself. (1939)

Section 3. Socialism and Communism.

Apart from their other characteristics, the outstanding thing about China's 600 million people is that they are 'poor and blank'. This may seem a bad thing, but in reality it is a good thing. Poverty gives rise to the desire for change, the desire for action and the desire for revolution. On a blank sheet of paper free from any mark, the freshest and most beautiful characters can be written, the freshest and most beautiful pictures can be painted. (1958)

Section 5. War and Peace.

Every Communist must grasp the truth, 'Political power grows out of the barrel of a gun.' (1938)

War, this monster of mutual slaughter among men, will be finally eliminated by the progress of human society, and in the not too distant future too. But there is only one way to eliminate it and that is to oppose war with war, to oppose counter-revolutionary war with revolutionary war, to oppose national counter-revolutionary war with national revolutionary war, and to oppose counter-revolutionary class war with revolutionary class war. . . . When human society advances to the point where classes and states are eliminated, there will be no more wars, counter-revolutionary or revolutionary, unjust or just; that will be the era of perpetual peace for mankind. Our study of the laws of revolutionary war springs from the desire to eliminate all wars; herein lies the distinction between us Communists and all the exploiting classes. (1936)

Section 6. Imperialism.

It is my opinion that the international situation has now reached a new turning point. There are two winds in the world today, the East Wind and the West Wind. There is a Chinese saying, 'Either the East Wind prevails over the West Wind or the West Wind prevails over the East Wind.' I believe it is characteristic of the situation today that the East Wind is prevailing over the West Wind. That is to say, the forces of socialism have become overwhelmingly superior to the forces of imperialism. (1957)

Section 9. The Mass Line.

The present upsurge of the peasant movement is a colossal event. In a very short time, in China's central, southern and northern provinces, several hundred million peasants will rise like a mighty storm, like a hurricane, a force so swift and violent that no power, however great, will be able to hold it back. They will smash all the trammels that bind them and rush forward along the road to liberation. They will sweep all the imperialists, warlords, corrupt officials, local tyrants and evil gentry into their graves. Every revolutionary party and every revolutionary comrade will be put to the test, to be accepted or rejected as they decide. There are three alternatives. To march at their head and lead them? To trail behind them, gesticulating and criticizing? Or to stand in their way and oppose them? Every Chinese is free to choose, but events will force you to make the choice quickly. (1927)

Section 12. Political Work

The atom bomb is a paper tiger which the U.S. reactionaries use to scare people. It looks terrible, but in fact it isn't. Of course, the atom bomb is a weapon of mass slaughter, but the outcome of a war is decided by the people, not by one or two new types of weapon. (1946)

Section 21. Self Reliance and Arduous Struggle

There is an ancient Chinese fable called 'The Foolish Old Man Who Removed the Mountains'. It tells of an old man who lived in northern China long, long ago and was known as the Foolish Old Man of North Mountain. His house faced south and beyond his doorway stood the two great peaks, Taihang and Wangwu, obstructing the way. With great determination he led his sons in digging up these mountains hoe in hand. Another greybeard, known as the Wise Old Man, saw them and said derisively, 'How silly of you to do this! It is quite impossible for you few to dig up these two huge mountains.' The Foolish Old Man replied, 'When I die, my sons will carry on; when they die, there will be my grandsons, and then their sons and grandsons, and so on to infinity. High as they are, the mountains cannot grow any higher and with every bit we dig, they will be that much lower. Why can't we clear them away?' Having refuted the Wise Old Man's view, he went on digging every day, unshaken in his conviction. God was moved by this, and he sent down two angels, who carried the mountains away on their backs. Today, two big mountains lie like a dead weight on the Chinese people. One is imperialism, the other is feudalism. The Chinese Communist Party has long made up its mind to dig them up. We must persevere and work unceasingly, and we, too, will touch God's heart. Our God is none other than the masses of the Chinese people. If they stand up and dig together with us, why can't these two mountains be cleared away? (1945)

Section 26. Discipline (deals with discipline of the Party and then makes eight points for attention)

The Eight Points for Attention are as follows:

(1) Speak politely.
(2) Pay fairly for what you buy.
(3) Return everything you borrow.
(4) Pay for anything you damage.
(5) Do not hit or swear at people.
(6) Do not damage crops.
(7) Do not take liberties with women.
(8) Do not ill-treat captives. (1947)

Section 28. Communists

A Communist should have largeness of mind and he should be staunch and active, looking upon the interests of the revolution as his very life and subordinating his personal interests to those of the revolution; always and everywhere he should adhere to principle and wage a tireless struggle against all incorrect ideas and actions, so as to consolidate the collective life of the Party and strengthen the ties between the Party and the masses; he should be more concerned about the Party and the masses than about any individual, and more concerned about others than about himself. Only thus can he be considered a Communist. (1937)

Section 30. Youth

The world is yours, as well as ours, but in the last analysis, it is yours. You young people, full of vigour and vitality, are in the bloom of life, like the sun at eight or nine in the morning. Our hope is placed on you. . . . The world belongs to you. . . . China's future belongs to you.

We must help all our young people to understand that ours is still a very poor country, that we cannot change this situation radically in a short time, and that only through the united efforts of our younger generation and all our people, working with their own hands, can China be made strong and prosperous within a period of several decades. The establishment of our socialist system has opened the road leading to the ideal society of the future, but to translate this ideal into reality needs hard work. (1957)

Section 33. Study

In order to have a real grasp of Marxism, one must learn it not only from books, but mainly through class struggle, through practical work and close contact with the masses of workers and peasants. When in addition to reading some Marxist books our intellectuals have gained some understanding through close contact with the masses of workers and peasants and through their own practical work, we will all be speaking the same language not only the common language of patriotism and the common language of the socialist system, but probably even the common language of the communist world outlook. If that happens, all of us will certainly work much better. (1957)

Index

Time Chart

EVENTS: IN JAPAN		IN CHINA	THE WORLD
	1500 BC	First written records	
Foundation of the Japanese Empire	600 BC		
	228-210 BC	Great Wall of China erected	
	207 BC	Han Dynasty founded	
	AD 868	First book printed from wood blocks	
Portuguese began trading with Japan	1542		
Spanish traders & missionaries arrived	1595		
	1601	First Catholic church in Peking	1600 East India Company granted sole rights to Eastern trade
Hostility to Christians: banned by Shogun (Hidetada)	1622		
Portuguese expelled	1638		
	1644-1912	Manchu Dynasty	1661, 1690 East India Company gained Bombay & Calcutta
	1715	East India Company trading post established in Canton	
Ban on Western books lifted	1716		
	1757	European merchants forbidden to trade at any port except Canton	1756-63 Britain & France at War in Europe, India and America
	1793	First British mission sent to China	1775 James Watt's steam engine
	1816	Second British mission sent to China	1776 American Declaration of Independence
	1833	Severe famine and plague	1789-1815 French Revolution & Napoleonic Wars
	1839-42	First Foreign (Opium) War & Treaties	1834 East India Company's monopoly ended
	1851-65	T'ai P'ing ('Long Hairs') Rebellion	
Matthew Perry landed in Japan; requested Commercial Treaty	1853		
Treaty of Kanagawa	1854		
	1854-60	Second Foreign War & Group of Treaties	1861 Russians tried to seize Tsushima
	1867	Meiji Rdestoration	
Japan adopted 'Westernization' policy	1868-71		
	1887	***Birth of Chiang Kai-Shek***	1883 French occupied Indo-China
Reforms & National Parliament established (1890)	**1893**	***Birth of Mao Tse-tung***	1891 Trans-Siberian Railway started
	1894	Dr. Sun Yat-sen started organizing revolutionary groups	
Sino-Japanese War	1894-5	Sino-Japanese War	
	1900-01	Boxer Rebellion	
Anglo-Japanese Alliance	1902		
Russo-Japanese War	1904-5	Era of Educational & Social Reforms	
	1908	Emperor Kuang Hsu died; Boy Emperor succeeded	